TWAYNE'S GREAT EDUCATORS SERIES

Samuel Smith, Ph. D.
Editor

ROUSSEAU AS EDUCATOR

3

JEAN JACQUES ROUSSEAU

Rousseau as Educator

MABEL LEWIS SAHAKIAN

Northeastern University

WILLIAM S. SAHAKIAN

Suffolk University

Twayne Publishers, Inc.   New York

Library of Congress Cataloging in Publication Data

Sahakian, Mabel Lewis.
  Rousseau as educator.

  (Twayne's great educators series)
  Bibliography: p.
  1. Rousseau, Jean Jacques, 1712-1778. 2. Education
—Philosophy. I. Sahakian, William S., joint author. II. Title.
Lb518.S33   370.1'092'4   73-20201
ISBN 0-8057-3589-5

MANUFACTURED IN THE UNITED STATES OF AMERICA

*Dedicated to our students who
listened to our lectures and
grappled with the ideas of
Jean Jacques Rousseau, citizen of Geneva*

Preface

Classics hold perennial interest for readers in all societies and in all generations. In studying Rousseau the reader is fortunate, for that great educator has several classics to his credit, both in social or political philosophy and in the philosophy of education.

In the following pages, the reader, after a preliminary overview of Rousseau's career, is offered in Chapter II an analytic discussion of his basic ideas concerning human nature and education. Chapter III deals with certain topics helpful to an understanding of Rousseau's major works: a synopsis of his views on civic education, a national system of education, and the education of a bored child, his indebtedness to John Locke, and educational conditions in France during Rousseau's lifetime. Chapters IV and V analyze his famous works in the philosophy of education, namely, *Julie, or the New Heloise* and *Emile,* respectively. The authors have endeavored to provide an integrated, coherent account of Rousseau's philosophy as expounded in these major works, but the reader should not be unduly alarmed when he comes upon apparent inconsistencies and paradoxes, for which Rousseau was notorious.

Two final Chapters VII and VIII have been supplied, one on the influence of Rousseau's ideas, the other on the critical reactions of scholars and the present authors to his philosophy of education. Chapter VIII emphasizes negative reactions, inasmuch as the positive influence of Rousseau is discussed in Chapter VII; furthermore, since the text as a whole is sympathetic to his ideas, negative comments and cautious evaluations complement the preceding discussion and should help the reader to gain insight into Rousseau's theories of education.

MABEL LEWIS SAHAKIAN

WILLIAM S. SAHAKIAN

Boston, Massachusetts

Contents

Preface

Chronology

1. Jean Jacques Rousseau, Citizen of Geneva   15

2. The Natural as the Criterion of Good   27

3. Prolegomena to Education according to Nature   42

4. *Julie, or the New Heloise*   61

5. *Emile* (Books I-IV)—Education as the Art of Forming Men   78

6. *Emile* (Book V)—Sophie: Education of an Ideal Woman   107

7. The Influence of Rousseau   118

8. Critical Reactions to Rousseau's Philosophy   123

Notes and References   141

Selected Bibliography of Rousseau's Writings   145

Selected Bibliography of Secondary Sources in English   147

Index   149

Chronology

1712   (June 28) Birth of Rousseau in Geneva

1722   Father's expatriation from Geneva (to Lyon)

1724   Rousseau's placement in the home of his uncle Bernard

1725   Apprenticeship to engraver in Geneva

1728   Flight from Geneva and beginning of Rousseau's wanderings
        Decisive meeting with Madame de Warens

1732-   Residence in the household of Madame de Warens
1737

1738   Journey to Montpellier (in company of Madame de Larnage)
        Beginning of studies in Chambéry

1740   Service as tutor to children of M. de Mably in Lyon

1741-   Residence in Paris
1756

1742   New system of musical notation rejected by Académie des sciences

1743   Appointment as secretary to French ambassador in Venice

1745   Liaison with Thérèse de Vasseur

1747   Composition of opera, *Les Muse Galantes*

1750   Publication of *Discourse on the Sciences and the Arts*

1752   Performance of Rousseau's operetta *Devin du village*

1754   Return to Geneva and the Protestant Church

1755   Publication of *Discourse on the Origin and the Foundations of Inequality among Men*
        Beginning of quarrel with Voltaire

1757   Residence at the Hermitage

1761	Publication of *Julie, or the New Heloise*
1762	Publication of *The Social Contract*
	Publication of *Emile*
	Condemnation of *Emile* by Paris parliament
1765-	Writing of *The Confessions*
1770	
1766	Arrival in England on invitation of David Hume
1767	Quarrel with Hume and return to France
1770	Final residence in Paris with Thérèse de Vasseur
1778	Death of Rousseau at Ermenonville
1781	Publication of *The Confessions*

Education is. . .the art of forming men.

Rousseau

CHAPTER 1

Jean Jacques Rousseau, Citizen of Geneva

The man for whom the people of Geneva showed their veneration by placing his statue on an island in Lake Geneva, Jean Jacques Rousseau, was born in that city in 1712. A half-century later he referred to this event in simple terms: "I was born in 1712 at Geneva, to Isaac Rousseau and Susanne Bernard, citizens."[1] He took pride in the fact that his parents were Genevan citizens. In his *The Confessions* (an autobiographical treatise published in 1781, posthumously), he claimed that his mother, who had died within a week as a consequence of his birth and for whose death he always felt a sense of guilt, was the daughter of the Protestant minister Bernard, but subsequent inquiry has disclosed that this statement was erroneous, as indeed were many other assertions in that uninhibited work of self-revelation. According to Rousseau, his father, a watchmaker and dancing-master, traced the paternal side of the family back to a Protestant bookseller of the mid-sixteenth century who had migrated from Paris to Geneva to escape the religious turmoil then prevailing in France. Unfortunately, owing to the absence of relevant documents, Rousseau's *The Confessions* remains the only source of substantial information about his antecedents and early childhood.

About the circumstances of his mother's death, he wrote:

"I cost my mother her life, and my birth was the first of my misfortunes," declaring that he had robbed his father of her companionship while himself entering the "world in almost dying condition."[2] The only other child was a brother, François, seven years his elder, whom Rousseau rarely saw, one who lapsed into "evil courses" and became a "profligate." François was abused by their father, beaten so severely on one occasion that Jean Jacques protected him from the blows by interposing his own body. Eventually the older boy ran away from home. Being the only son left in the household, Jean Jacques took advantage of the overindulgent treatment accorded him by his irresponsible, violent-tempered, pleasure-loving father and a highly emotional, impulsive aunt whose lack of self-control appears to have inspired similar tendencies in the boy.

I *Early Childhood*

Rousseau wrote candidly about his early childhood experiences. He recalled being loved by everyone, even though he was "a babbler, a glutton, and, sometimes, a liar." He was not permitted to roam the streets like other children but lived a sheltered life permeated with gentleness and affection. He gave credit to his aunt for stimulating in him a passion for music, an interest that remained with him throughout his career. Yet he recalled her immaturity, her childish and harsh discipline which had an adverse effect upon his character, and he deplored the maltreatment of children then in vogue.

Rousseau's father was his first teacher and taught him to read at an early age, but failed to inculcate in the boy habits of self-discipline either by means of persuasion or example. Together they read and discussed amusing books and romances left in the home library by the mother. Father and son shared a spirit of flighty impulsiveness and sentimentality. On one occasion, cited by Rousseau, their conversation about his mother left them weeping uncontrollably. The child read classics, such as Plutarch's *Lives,* Ovid's *Metamorphoses,* and some works of Molière. In 1720 when Jean Jacques was only eight years old, his father became involved in a violent quarrel with a French army captain and was sentenced to a short term in prison which he avoided by escaping to Lyon. The boy was sent to live with an uncle, Bernard, who then arranged to transfer him to the school of a Protestant minister, Lambercier, at Bossey, a village outside Geneva. There he was expected to learn "with Latin, all the petty rubbish that attends the name of education."

II *Apprenticeships*

In 1724 he returned to the home of his uncle Bernard and was apprenticed to a lawyer (named Masseron) in order "to learn the useful trade of *fee-grabber*," as Rousseau opprobriously referred to the legal profession. The lawyer adjudged the boy a failure and sent him back to his uncle; the following year he was again apprenticed, this time to an engraver (named Ducommun), "a rough and violent young man" from whom he fled three years later, claiming that he had been cruelly abused by him. It seems that a specific incident brought an abrupt end to the second apprenticeship. The master had warned Rousseau about severe punishment if he failed to return home from the city at night before the gates closed, and when this happened he ran away and chose to become "a tramp" rather than suffer further mistreatment at the hands of the engraver. Rousseau blamed Ducommun for having taught him the vices of idleness, lying, and thievery. Referring to this period of apprenticeships (1723-1728), he wrote: "Thus the most precious time of my adolescence was lost in silliness before my destiny had been decided upon."[3]

Rousseau reluctantly considered the possibility of going back to his father or to his former teacher, Lambercier. But an unhappy meeting revealed that his father "no longer found in me his idol," and he felt that Lambercier would not welcome a pupil who had failed to live up to expectations. He rarely saw his father thereafter and never again met with Lambercier. In his autobiography he noted reasons for his feeling of rejection, citing defects of character he attributed to deprivation and poverty, which whetted his appetite for sensuality and for improper dispositons. He cited the analogous effect of dismissing children from the dining table when the most appetizing dishes are being served, thus training them to be gluttons and thieves, and explained that he himself "became in a short time both one and the other." Elaborating, he confessed to excessive sensuality but not to the extremes of gluttony, analyzing himself as a shy individual possessing strong passions which frequently deprived him of a sense of discretion so that he acted in a shamelessly impudent, reckless, cynical, and violent manner. He was not motivated by the desire for wealth or material comforts; money meant less to him than it does to most people. He recalled that he had received a "reasonable and virtuous education," including religious training, and added: "I was never a real child. I always felt and thought as a man. It was only when I grew up that I settled into my proper age."

III *Meeting with Madame Warens*

In 1728, shortly after the Ducommun incident, Rousseau followed an unsettled style of life—incessant traveling, shifting about from one type of employment to another and finding himself unfit for any of them—until he achieved fame more than three decades later as a man of letters. His first stop was at Confignon, about two leagues from Geneva, where, hungry and penniless, he was proselytized into the Roman Catholic faith by M. de Pontverre, a zealous priest who effected the conversion at a dinner complete with wine. "Far from thinking of returning me to my home," he recalled, "he took advantage of my desire to escape from it and made it impossible for me to return even if I should wish to do so."[4] M. de Pontverre informed Rousseau that God was calling him to go to Annecy and directed him to a recent proselyte residing there named Madame de Warens. The fateful meeting with her (she was a widow twenty-eight years of age) took place on Palm Sunday in 1728 as she was making her way to the holiday service in church. "This moment" (Rousseau wrote fifty years afterward) "was decisive for my whole life and affected through an inevitable chain of circumstances the destiny of my days."[5] The widow's life story paralleled Rousseau's in that she, too, had lost her mother at birth and had acquired an education spasmodically from a variety of sources. She had benefited from instruction and guidance provided by her governess, father, employers, and especially lovers. She was quite willing to support Rousseau, who had been attracted to her at their very first meeting. Despite bonds of mutual affection, however, gossip about their relationship impelled him to give up their association.

IV *Episodes in Turin*

Across the Alps in Turin there was a monastery which accepted many converts to Catholicism. Rousseau went there to receive the religious indoctrination required for induction into the Roman Catholic Church. He arrived in the busy metropolis with only a little pocket money, of which some newly found acquaintances easily relieved him; he later recalled that a Madame Sabran "managed to get everything from me." In the monastery, on presenting his letters of introduction, he was "conducted to the hospice for catechumens, to be instructed in the religion with which I was to purchase my livelihood." Among other neophytes were "rascals" and "sluts" who found the arrangements to be worthwhile from a practical point of view. After nine days in residence, Rousseau, with edifying pomp, was inducted into the church, and then, with twenty francs in his possession, he took to the streets.

Even the most frugal mode of living soon threatened to empty his purse and therefore, while waiting hopefully for some more profitable opportunity to materialize, he went about offering his services as an engraver to local shops at low prices and was even willing to allow a prospective customer to decide the amount of payment. But these efforts were unsuccessful until one shopkeeper's wife, Madame Basile, who was about a half-dozen years his senior, agreed out of compassion to give him room and board in her establishment in exchange for his professional services. She managed the shop with the help of a clerk whenever her husband was traveling on business journeys. On one occasion, however, when the husband came home he learned from the clerk that Rousseau had been making indiscreet advances to

Madame Basile, whereupon Rousseau was immediately dismissed.

Following termination of this "first love adventure," and with funds nearly exhausted, he was compelled to accept employment as a servant or footman in the household of Comtesse de Vercellis to whom he had been referred by a sympathetic landlady. He described his status as that of one who was "obliged to be a servant to her servants" in that household.

It was there also that the famous theft incident occurred which was to trouble his conscience for the remainder of his days and became the principal motivation for writing *The Confessions*. He had been employed only a few months when the Comtesse de Vercellis died and a great deal of confusion arose during the settlement of her affairs. There was much concern about the problem of accounting for all items in the estate. During the confusion, Rousseau stole an old red-and-silver-colored ribbon and kept it among his personal belongings, where it was soon found by the staff alerted to the missing article by the meticulous person in charge of these matters. When they questioned Rousseau and asked for an explanation, he became flustered and blurted out that Marion the cook had given the ribbon to him. Marion, a fine young girl of impeccable reputation who had done no harm to Rousseau, stood astonished before her accuser as he insisted that she was the guilty one. The result was that both of them were promptly dismissed.

His cowardly role in this incident troubled Rousseau's conscience throughout the years and caused him many sleepless nights. Reporting the incident decades later in *The Confessions*, he wrote: "The Comte de la Roque, in dismissing the two of us, contented himself with saying that the conscience of the guilty person sufficiently vindicates the innocent. His prediction has not been in vain; it fulfills itself every day."[6] Rousseau was convinced that his false accusation had prevented the girl from obtaining respectable employment; time and again he devoted sleepless hours at night to vivid recollections of her plight and he was never able to unburden his conscience, not even by confessing his guilt to a friend. In *The Confessions*, written so long afterward, he commented:

"This cruel remembrance troubles and demolishes me at times to the point that, unable to sleep, I envision that poor girl coming to reproach me for my crime as if it had been committed only yesterday. . . . This burden has rested on my conscience to this day without easing, and I state that the desire to free myself therefrom in some way has been largely responsible for my decision to write my confessions."[7]

For a short period after the preceding incident, Rousseau was able to meet bare living expenses out of modest severance pay he had received from the Vercellis estate. Eventually he found it necessary to accept employment in the household of the Comte de Gouvon, again in the degrading capacity of a lackey. This time, however, he encountered a bit of good fortune when the master's son, the Abbé de Gouvon, on learning that Rousseau knew Latin, volunteered to instruct him in other disciplines. "Thus by one of those oddities which have so often occurred in the course of my life, I was pupil and lackey in the same house, and though but a servant, had a teacher whose birthright would have qualified him for that office even with the children of kings."[8] It is probable that he was being trained to be a confidential secretary, but, unfortunately, once more his bad judgment and tactless behavior soon resulted in his dismissal.

V *The Madame de Warens Affair*

At this critical juncture, having kept in touch with Madame de Warens during his stay in Turin, Rousseau turned his thoughts and steps toward her. On his arrival he was warmly received and quite pleased when he overheard a conversation in which she remarked: "Let them say what they will; seeing that Providence returns him to me, I am determined not to abandon him." Defying the gossips, she put him up in her drawing room. They had pet names for each other, "Little one" for him, "Mamma" for her, terms not justified by any difference in their ages which was an insignificant factor at their prime stage of adulthood.

Thus in 1730 Rousseau enjoyed living with Mamma. Eventually, being interested in his career, she made arrangements for him to enroll in the St. Lazare Seminary at Annecy to become a priest. "I was destined," he recalled, "to be the rubbish of all professions." But the Superior formed a negative judgment about his character and sent him back to Madame de Warens "as an individual that was not even good enough to be a priest."

Undaunted by his failure at the seminary, Mamma arranged for him to be tutored in music by a Parisian, M. Le Maître, choirmaster in the cathedral. Rousseau studied music for six months secluded in the choirmaster's house except for visits from Mamma and trips to attend church services. Suddenly, during Passion week in 1730, M. Le Maître quarreled with the Abbé de Vidonne and simply disappeared, leaving the clergy in the lurch during this vitally important period of the Christian year. He went off to Lyon with Rousseau who had been told by Mamma to remain at his side, ostensibly in order to assist him professionally, although her real purpose was to rescue Rousseau from the influence of M. Venture, a new, undesirable companion.

At Lyon an unhappy incident occurred in which Rousseau was guilty of reprehensible conduct, as he admitted in the *Confessions,* adding that if he had any more such painful episodes to report, he would abandon the entire task of writing the autobiography. It seems that his companion, M. Le Maître, fell down in a violet epileptic fit and lay senseless and foaming at the mouth in the road. Rousseau was terrified by the sight and screamed for assistance, calling out for someone to take the man to his inn, but then he himself turned the corner and disappeared, "abandoning the only friend on whom he could count." No one knew of his cowardly behavior, but it disturbed him greatly and became the subject of what he called his "third painful confession." After the incident at Lyon he returned to Annecy eager for the warmth and tenderness of Mamma; only to find on arriving that she had left for Paris.

For some months he tramped about from place to place, teaching music at Lausanne and Neuchâtel, working as a secretary, becoming involved in improbable adventures reported only in his own statements. In 1732 he made his way from Paris to Savoy on foot, having learned that Madame de

Warens was in Chambéry, and most of the time until 1741 maintained a close relationship with Mamma. In 1736 she took a country house, Les Charmettes, near that city; Rousseau enjoyed living there in summer, returning to the city in winter. But he was quite ill at the time, an illness which marked a turning point in his life since, during its course, he began methodical study of literature and science. He read Voltaire's *Philosophical Letters* which gave him a thirst for knowledge never extinguished. He became acquainted with the Lockean-Cartesian philosophical controversy and also read the works of Montaigne, the Port Royalists, and Fénelon, among others. He was ill again in 1738 and journeyed to Montpellier for this reason, but taking with him a female companion, Madame de Larnage. On returning he found another gentleman installed in Les Charmettes, so not long thereafter he accepted a position as private tutor to the children of M. de Mably of Lyon, a brief, unsatisfactory experience but one which inspired him with a lifelong interest in education. He went back again to Les Charmettes for a brief visit with Mamma in 1741 but, noting that she was quite content with her other male companion, he left again, this time for Paris, ending the relationship with Madame de Warens. (He did not see her again until 1754 on a visit to Geneva.)

VI *Rousseau in Paris*

In Paris Rousseau presented to the Academy of Sciences a new but impractical system of musical notation using numbers to indicate the main elements of music such as notes, keys, rests, octaves, measures, and time. However, since a monk named Souhaitte had already invented a similar method as applied to the musical scale, Rousseau's system failed to win approval when the Academy considered it in August, 1742. Fortunately, he was assisted by influential, wealthy people whom he had met, particularly Madame Dupin and her stepson, M. de Franceuil, who became two of his best friends. She obtained an appointment for Rousseau in 1743 as secretary to the French ambassador in Venice. This position lasted about eighteen months, ending in a quarrel with the ambassador and Rousseau's return to Paris in 1745, where he copied music for fees and also earned a small stipend as secretary to Madame Dupin and M. de Franceuil. He met Diderot, d'Alembert, and other literary lights and contributed articles on music to Diderot's great Encyclopédie.

Rousseau had met a servant girl, Thérèse le Vasseur, unattractive, uneducated, but whose simplicity of manner appealed to him, and she became his mistress. According to his *Confessions,* she bore him five children, all of whom he promptly consigned on birth to a home for foundlings. Although he felt at that time that this was the right course of action, in later years he sincerely regretted it. When he became a famous writer, enemies condemned him for neglecting the "sacred duties of paternity" but there is even doubt that he ever saw the children, and their existence may have been a hoax by Thérèse and her mother to keep their hold on him. At any rate, although the mother-in-law was the bane of his existence, he felt happy with Thérèse, manifested a singular devotion to her throughout his life, and referred to her as "the only true consolation that heaven has granted me, in my misery." Between them there was little more in common than an emotional attachment, for she lacked intellectual capacity to understand the depth of his ideas and spirit, and her permanent relationship to him remained that of housekeeper to a real stranger.

Rousseau's literary career which speedily made him famous was launched in 1750 with the publication of his *Discourse on the Sciences and the Arts,* an essay previously awarded a prize by the Academy of Dijon. In this essay he condemned all institutions of civilization and paid tribute to the morals and customs of the simple, natural life of the ancients. He also wrote a supplement to the first essay, *Discourse on the Origin and the Foundations of Inequality among Men,* contending that primitive, natural man had been corrupted by the greed for power and property, resulting in the evils of gross inequality, immorality, and oppression. (The supplement, which failed to win a prize offered by the Academy at Dijon, was published in 1755 shortly before Rousseau left Paris.) Another of his creative works was the opera, *Le Devin du village,* performed successfully before Louis XV at Fontainebleau in 1752. Music critics praised it, but he refused to be presented at court and thereby lost a royal pension.

VII *Last Works of Rousseau*

The year 1756 found Rousseau and Thérèse living in the Hermitage, a small country home belonging to Madame d'Épinay with whose sister-in-law, Madame d'Huodetot, he fell in love although she, for her part, with her own husband and another lover on hand, was not too enthusiastic about the relationship. Before long he quarreled with his friends at the Hermitage and made his departure in the winter of 1757-1758, residing for a time at Montlouis nearby.

While at the Hermitage in 1756-1757 Rousseau had written one of his major works, *Julie, or the New Heloise (Julie, ou la nouvelle Héloïse,* published in 1761), a partly autobiographical novel which attributes character defects and evil deeds not to the individuals involved but to the pressures and institutions of society. He also wrote the *Letter to d'Alembert on the Theater* (published in 1758) which criticized Voltaire and aroused his enmity. Thereafter he devoted himself to writing two of his most influential masterpieces: *The Social Contract* (a defense of individual rights and democratic government, published in 1762); and *Emile,* a semiautobiographical novel illustrating and discussing his theories on the ideal education of children and youth (published in 1762).

The preceding works became immensely popular but were bitterly assailed by conservative interests and official circles. The *New Heloise* was attacked as immoral owing to the ideas in its love story. *The Social Contract* offended all adherents of the monarchical form of government, which Rousseau characterized as government by "petty cheats, burglars, and intriguers." The *Emile* advocated new ideals for a Deist, individualized education to replace the wretched system of education prevailing in the artificial society of the time, and therefore antagonized the Church and many other defenders of the status quo. From the time of publication to this day, however, this epochal work has exerted enormous influence on educational theory and practice; in fact, Rousseau's ideas eventually became the basis for many of the modern movements in education developed in democratic nations of the Western world.

Condemnation of *Emile* by the Paris parliament in 1762, following reports that he was to be arrested, impelled Rousseau to flee the country. He went to live in Switzerland. When the Council of Geneva also condemned the book, he renounced his citizenship and attacked the Council as well as the Genevan constitution in his *Letters on the Mount* (1763). Meanwhile his relations with the previously sympathetic Encyclopedists had been strained to the breaking point. Therefore, beset with personal and professional quarrels, afflicted by illness and persecution for his beliefs, he settled in Neuchâtel under the protection of Frederick II, King of Prussia. But his views aroused wide opposition and controversies. Again he became a fugitive, lived for a short time on the Isle of St. Pierre until ordered to leave by the Bernese government and then went to England upon the invitation of the philosopher David Hume. He soon quarreled with Hume and went back to France in 1767, where he moved about from one place to another until he finally settled in Paris in 1770. While in England he had written a large part of his *The Confessions*. His last years were devoted to several works: his masterpiece of autobiography, *The Confessions;* his *Dialogues;* and his *Reveries*. The final decade of his life was troubled by a persecution mania reflecting memories of hardships, quarrels, and political opponents. He died suddenly in 1778 in a country home he had rented at Ermenonville, outside Paris.

CHAPTER 2

The Natural as the Criterion of Good

Permeating the writings of Rousseau is the decisive role accorded therein to nature, to whatever is *natural*. Rousseau viewed all of reality and every discipline—whether it be social philosophy, education, political theory, or religious philosophy—by reference to natural processes. His criterion for determining what is right and good, as well as what is true, is the degree of conformity to nature, to natural forces. Consequently, for Rousseau the only good man is the natural man, the only good education is the natural education, the only good society is the natural society, and the only true religion is the natural religion. He accepts as infallible the premise that *nature is right*.

What, then, in human experience is natural? What is unnatural? Rousseau was consistently positive about one fact, namely, the fact that his contemporary civilization was unnatural, a composite of evil, artificial institutions and customs contrary to beneficent nature. In the opening paragraphs of several books, he affirms this basic conclusion. One reads in *The Social Contract:* "Man is born free and everywhere he is in chains"; and the preamble to *Emile* declares: "God makes all things good; man meddles with them and they become evil."[1] "Natural man is good," he wrote in the appendix to his essay on the origin of inequality.

Although Rousseau's writings are inconsistent and sometimes rambling, they form an integrated whole. He himself
pointed out in a letter to Malesherbes that three of his
writings—*Discourse on the Sciences and the Arts, Discourse
on the Origin and the Foundations of Inequality among Men,*
and *Emile*—are inseparable works intended to convey different aspects of the same point of view or message. To these he
probably should have added *The Social Contract,* published
in 1762 a month or two before *Emile.* In order fully to appreciate Rousseau's philosophy of education, therefore, one
must take all these writings into account. Anyone who
wishes to understand clearly the fundamental theories espoused in *Emile* concerning the nature and purpose of education must also gain an understanding of Rousseau's political,
social, and religious philosophy as well as his philosophical
anthropology, his philosophy of man.

I *The Meaning of Natural Man*

Rousseau's philosophy of education opposes the establishment and calls for a return to nature because civilization is
corrupt. Truth can be found only "in nature, which never
lies."[2] Nature is always right.

But this argument begs the questions: What is nature?
What is natural? Certain plausible answers are rejected by
Rousseau. He does not accept the proposition that (1) animal
desires and their satisfaction are man's sole good, nor that
(2) nature is the same thing for man as for other animals,
nor that (3) reversion to a state of savagery is the truly
natural course of action. Nature requires art in order to be
cultivated, to be perfected. It is culture that makes the individual more natural, but in the culture he must avoid any
art that denatures him. Nature must be viewed as if it were
a germ that comes to fruition. The germ to be cultivated is
found in civilized man and savage alike, and the process of
its development involves both conscious and unconscious
forces. Art is necessary to develop these basic forces of nature. "Let us lay it down as an incontrovertible rule that the
first impulses of nature are always right."[3]

II *Back to Nature*

Since civilization in its present form is corrupt, it behooves one to return to his primal nature and remain attuned to it. Culture should comport with the primal principles, for man is natural only when he is true to his own nature. This is a most difficult task, owing to the probability that no person has ever been entirely natural in every aspect of his existence. It is a mistake to assume that the man who lives in accord with nature must be a savage. In Rousseau's writings such a man is portrayed as the finest of philosophers, even though an occasional passage may seem to be inconsistent with this view. But critics who interpret Rousseau's ideas as if they equate natural living with a permanent condition of savagery, or art with retrogression, are guilty of the fallacy of vicious abstraction. When Rousseau referred to natural man, he had much more than a mere savage in mind.

In order for the individual to attain the fullest growth and development, said Rousseau, it is necessary to make use of the right art which is found in the root impulses of human nature. Rousseau's faith in human nature is tantamount to faith in God, for if a human being's nature were askew, then God would be in error. Nature is right; hence a man's primal nature is good.

III *Self-love and Sympathy*

In the original nature of each person there is a reservoir of self-love and sympathy, the former of which is an instinct of self-preservation, while the latter functions as a gregarious instinct and attitude of mutual aid. Humanity would have perished long ago had it not been for self-preservation impulses; and if men had not been endowed with sympathy, they would have destroyed each other. Since these two instincts are fundamental to human nature, it follows that subsequent growth stems from them. Love of self and love of kind are two guiding instincts—good instincts which precede reason. But these good instincts cannot be said to be moral, for morality depends upon reason to determine the proper objective of an act. Hence goodness precedes morality. Every aspect of a person's education is contingent upon his nature; consequently it is important both to know human nature and to know that it is good.

Rousseau contradicts the interpretation of human nature expounded by Thomas Hobbes, the English philosopher who viewed human nature as corrupt, noxious, belligerent, and dissident. In the nature of man, according to Hobbes,

we find three principal causes of quarrel. First, competition, secondly, diffidence, thirdly, glory. . .

Hereby it is manifest, that during the time men live without a common power to keep them all in awe, they are in that condition which is called war; and such a war, as is of every man, against every man. For war, consists not in battle only, or the act of fighting; but in a tract of time, wherein the will to contend by battle is sufficiently known. . . . So the nature of war, consists not in actual fighting, but in the known disposition thereto, during all the time there is no assurance to the contrary. All other time is peace.[4]

It was the contention of Hobbes that morality does not exist until law is enacted, that is, until a social contract is instituted, since man's natural state is one of corruption and belligerence. Rousseau disputed this argument as follows:

Let us not conclude, with Hobbes, that because man has no idea of goodness, he must be naturally wicked; that he is vicious because he does not know virtue; that he always refuses to do his fellow-creatures services which he does not think they have a right to demand; or that by virtue of the right he truly claims to everything he needs, he foolishly imagines himself the sole proprietor of the whole universe. Hobbes had seen clearly the defects of all the modern definitions of natural right: but the consequences which he deduces from his own show that he understands it in an equally false sense. In reasoning on the principles he lays down, he ought to have said that the state of nature, being that in which the care for our own preservation is the least prejudicial to that of others, was consequently the best calculated to promote peace, and the most suitable for mankind.[5]

Rousseau had another objection to the Hobbesian view of human nature:

There is another principle which has escaped Hobbes; which, having been bestowed on mankind, to moderate, on certain occasions, the impetuosity of egoism, or, before its birth, the desire of self-preservation, tempers the ardour with which he pursues his own welfare, by an innate repugnance at seeing a fellow-creature suffer. I think I need not fear contradiction in holding man to be possessed of the only natural virtue, which could not be denied him by the most violent detractor of human virtue. I am speaking of compassion.[6]

Nevertheless, Rousseau and Hobbes were in basic agreement that a person's fundamental drive is self-preservation. In Rousseau's view, however, it was not the human being's primal instincts that presented a problem, for Hobbes erred in assuming that after their inception these instincts went astray and impelled men to do evil. Whereas for Hobbes, morality originates with law, for Rousseau it originates with reason.

Repudiating the notion of original sin, Rousseau held that "the only natural passion is self-love or selfishness taken in a wider sense. This selfishness is good in itself."[7] It is good because it preserves one's life. "Our passions are the chief means of self-preservation; to try to destroy them is therefore as absurd as it is useless; this would be to overcome nature, to reshape God's handiwork." Thus the origin of our passions, wrote Rousseau, the roots and spring of all the rest, the only attribute which is born with man, which never leaves him so long as he lives, is self-love. "Self-love is always good, always in accordance with the order of nature."[8]

IV *The Role of Conscience*

Conscience, too, plays a role. Instincts of love of self and of sympathy (love for others) occasionally conflict, with a necessity arising for mitigation, compromise, and concession. The sentiment of conscience stems from this process of mitigation, compromise, and reciprocal concession. Consequently, conscience, instead of being a product of education, is a derivative of the human being's fundamental instincts. Although conscience is natural and older than reason, it becomes a moral entity only when reason, which directs the will toward moral conduct, begins to do its work. Inasmuch as conscience itself is natural, it is good.

Conscience, being only a sentiment, however, is blind and requires the good offices of reason for enlightenment. A person becomes moral because reason distinguishes right from wrong and directs him toward prescribed objectives, thereby transforming his innate goodness into virtue. "Reason alone teaches us to know good and evil," wrote Rousseau in *Emile*. "Therefore conscience, which makes us love the one and hate the other, though it is independent of reason, cannot develop without it." He added, "Before the age of reason we do good or ill without knowing it, and there is no morality in our actions, although there is sometimes in our feeling with regard to other people's actions in relation to ourselves. A child wants to overturn everything he sees. He breaks and smashes everything he can reach; he seizes a bird as he seizes a stone, and strangles it without knowing what he is about."[9] Motivation toward right and hatred of wrong stem from the moral force of conscience, an innate sentiment. Thus, while reason provides the moral guide, conscience exerts the moral force.

Because conscience invariably loves what is right and never loves what is wrong, it is infallible; it errs only when it mistakes right actions for wrong actions. But that act of judgment is the task of reason, although the fallibility of reason is everywhere quite apparent. Inasmuch as reason validates the sentiment of conscience, virtue results from the perfect union of reason and conscience. "Extend self-love to others and it is transformed into virtue."[10]

V *The Role of Reason*

Occasionally charged with irrationalism or antirationalism, Rousseau nevertheless did accord to reason an important role. Although conscience is a primal, older attribute, reason is a necessary and desirable one, necessary and desirable for educating and developing human nature. Reason runs amok, however, when it follows its own artificial fancies instead of the primal nature of man. Civilization and education have committed two major blunders: (1) ignoring man's primal nature and (2) cultivating an unsound culture that is not based on the native propensities of the human being. Reason should remain within its circumscribed bounds by seeing to the development of a person's nature, for that is both the rational and the responsible function of true reason. "It is reason that engenders self-respect, and reflection that confirms it."[11] Nature has provided man with sentiments, while reason has shaped them to suit man's fancy. Culture, then, is the work of reason operating upon a blend of sentiments.

The properly educated man is one whose primal sentiments remain undistorted and unrepressed by reason, and hence retains his natural state in contrast to the unnatural man with his distorted and suppressed sentiments. Such is the state of the naked savage whose condition is preferable to that of a distorted philosopher. A primitive, natural personality is preferable to a cultivated, unnatural one. When one's only choice is between ignorance and error, the former is preferable. Accordingly it is not the savage but the natural man properly developed that is Rousseau's ideal. "When I want to train a natural man, I do not want to make him a savage and send him back to the woods."[12]

VI *Negative Education*

Apparently influenced by the ancient Greek philosophers, especially Socrates and Plato, Rousseau viewed education as the process of bringing to consciousness what lies dormant in the unconscious. Education should allow the natural impulse to proceed and take its natural course, thus preventing artificial, immoral influences. One must not think of education as offering the child a content or of creating in him or even instilling in him something that was not initially there, something out of nothing.

The role of education is to provide the best possible conditions for permitting the innate propensity to filter through, to express itself and develop. Accordingly education is keynoted by the negative so that a child's innate talents, his original nature, is activated and cultivated. The negative principle governing education, that of preventing artificial influences, must be implemented most scrupulously during the early stages of the child's education. Just as good hygiene is the most protective and negative consideration in medicine, preventing illness, so in education there is a comparable protective and negative factor, namely, the encouragement of native tendencies, preventing artificiality and distorted personality.

Rousseau's theory of negative education is bound up closely with his doctrine of innate goodness. If children are good by nature, the wise course to follow in education is to allow them to develop as naturally as possible, and not to adulterate nature with unnatural and foreign elements produced by civilization. The faults prevalent among children are the deleterious effects of improper education, and they are not found within the child but have been injected from without, infecting him with the poisons of civilization and culture. Consequently the principle of negativity in education must be carefully observed as a protective means of excluding from education all those artificial influences of civilization that may prove damaging to the child's wholesome development.

Not only did Rousseau's philosophy of education denigrate civilization, but his premise concerning the native goodness of man negated the Christian Church doctrine of original sin. Furthermore, his philosophy of education not only excluded religious influences from early childhood but also advocated entrusting education to the public instead of to the clergy. In a pastoral letter the Archbiship of Paris expressed the adverse reactions of the Church to such educational theories. Not that Rousseau was entirely opposed to religion, since he believed that religious belief should be a matter of natural unfolding as an integral part of the self, but the intrusion of dogma which he regarded as an artificial product of civilization was offensive to him. In his view the process of education should aim to permit every natural impulse to unfold, while at the same time preventing artificial external influences from perverting the innate, good dispositions which constitute the original nature of a human being. He insisted that education should filter out obnoxious external elements tending to impede or distort the process of natural development. Since he felt certain that the fundamental instincts of the individual are good, he held steadfast to his faith in the natural goodness of all men.

Negative education possessed still another value. Since a child's nature—his genius and talents—is not immediately apparent but discloses itself gradually, education should be negative, a process of observation instead of an attempt to impose subject matter upon the child.

Negative education is difficult to administer because it requires both alertness to the child's peculiar talents and competence in suitably arranging conditions so as to permit natural development to take its course, its motto being: in doing all one does nothing. This principle does not mean that the educator is unnecessary or that his presence is not desirable. On the contrary, he should be ever present but unnoticeably, giving the pupil the impression of being on his own, of functioning autonomously instead of merely carrying out the wishes of the instructor. Often a skillful teacher will be able to anticipate what the child is about to say, and he must then immerse himself in the program of activities which the child has selected for himself. Self-control is therefore an essential qualification of a good teacher, who must be constantly active in connection with his pupil's enterprise. The career of teaching, said Rousseau, is indeed a difficult one.

The good teacher is on constant watch to see that class instruction does not repress his pupil's individuality. This task is so time-consuming that there should be only one pupil assigned to every teacher. For this reason public education of pupils in groups is not feasible. (Note that Rousseau eventually modified this view and advocated free public education for citizenship.) Education should also be free of preconceived notions or prejudices rife in the community. False beliefs and prejudices vary with different societies. The child who is not taught any such myths will see that they are not identical or universal and will become an independent thinker.

VII *Education as Re-education*

Strange, is it not, that people are not natural? Man, basically good, has been developed or educated badly. Apparently something has gone amiss, for each person, born with love of self and sympathy for others and then endowed with a conscience guided by reason toward goodness, has nevertheless succeeded in perverting himself. What, then, is the explanation?

One reason is perverted self-love, an aberration that is recognized as pride. Love of self requires only that one's needs be satisfied, but when it is permitted to degenerate into greed, pride, envy, and vainglory so that one seeks to accumulate more than other people do, love transforms itself into pride. Needs stemming from love of self are simple. If it is not possible for two persons to share certain possessions, one can easily defer to the other out of sympathy. While pride in individuals makes them strive to snatch up all things, the love of self motivates them to pursue only what is required. "Savage man, when he has dined, is at peace with all nature, and the friend of all his fellow-creatures." With respect to civilized man, however, the situation is not the same.

The case is quite different with man in the state of society, for whom first necessaries have to be provided, and then superfluities; delicacies follow next, then immense wealth, then subjects, and then slaves. He enjoys not a moment's relaxation; and what is yet stranger, the less natural and pressing his wants, the more head-strong are his passions, and, still worse, the more he has it in his power to gratify them; so that after a long course of prosperity, after having swallowed up treasures and ruined multitudes, the hero ends up by cutting every throat till he finds himself, at last, sole master of the world. Such is in miniature the moral picture, if not of human life, at least of the secret pretensions of the heart of civilized man.[13]

In advocating a return to nature, Rousseau had in mind the ideal that each person would renounce all illusory needs created by pride but would know and provide for his genuine, natural needs; in so doing he would reject false or distorted benefits and would discover the basic needs of his true self. He differentiated between mental and physical needs. "The mind, as well as the body, has its needs: those of the body are the basis of society, those of the mind its ornaments."[14] Sometimes it requires a "revolution to bring men back to common sense."

Education, said Rousseau, has not served civilization well, for "the arts and sciences owe their birth to our vices." Reviewing the origins of the arts and sciences, he concluded that "astronomy was born of superstition, eloquence of ambition, hatred, falsehood and flattery; geometry of avarice; physics of an idle curiosity; and even moral philosophy of human pride."[15] Examining the evil origins of civilization, he asked: "What would become of the arts, were they not cherished by luxury? If men were not unjust, of what use were jurisprudence? What would become of history, if there were no tyrants, wars, or conspiracies?"[16]

Education, wealth, and conveniences, instead of fostering the good life, contribute adverse consequences. "As the conveniences of life increase, as the arts are brought to perfection, and luxury spreads, true courage flags, the virtues disappear; and this is the effect of the sciences and of those arts which are exercised in the privacy of men's dwellings."[17] Luxury and leisure are disguised ills, for "to live without doing some good is a great evil in the political as well as in the moral world; and hence every useless citizen should be regarded as a pernicious person."[18]

Education and the institutions of civilization have been ordered according to pride. "The first man who, having enclosed a piece of ground, bethought himself of saying *This is mine,* and found people simple enough to believe him, was the real founder of civil society."[19] As the race began to impute value to objects, intended injuries became an affront. Rousseau cited with approval Locke's statement, "There can be no injury, where there is no property."[20]

Education has indeed not served man well. "Had he gone back to the state of nature, his inquiries would clearly have had a different result, and man would have been seen to be subject to very few evils not of his own creation. . . . Man is naturally good. What, then, can have depraved him to such an extent, except the changes in his constitution that have occurred, the advances he has made and the knowledge he has acquired?"[21] Human society has taught people to hate one another in proportion to their clash of interests and to do mischief surreptitiously to each other.

VIII *Childhood and Education*

Childhood is a genuine experience, a *sui generis,* a period of life that must not be treated as a merely preparatory interval. The tutor must not interfere in this period with a pompous air of authority, but must approach the entire enterprise of education negatively.

Rousseau insisted that the child should be reared in the most natural ways with utter freedom from restraint. He brought back into fashion the practice of breast-feeding as every child's birthright. He condemned the custom of swaddling the infant's feet so as to inhibit free movement. He held that instruction in reading and writing should follow the child's interest in learning these skills, should not be undertaken prior to such interest, and should not consist of artificial lessons but should be based on his sensory contacts with nature. The child should not learn from books and sermons but from real things, the book of nature, by means of his own activities and creations, not the subject matter and devices prepared in advance by educators. Instead of required tasks, self-directed activities should be encouraged.

It must not be concluded that Rousseau advocated indulging, coddling, or spoiling the child, for, as he pointed out, nature has built-in provisions guarding against these consequences of self-direction. Often the child will make mistakes which may be painful, but pain is nature's sanction, and he should be permitted to cry, provided that it is not caused by a need requiring attention. Stoical endurance is desirable because it nurtures freedom; one should therefore allow the child to endure the cold and rest his head on a pillow that is not too soft and comfortable, but hard. Freedom, because it contributes to independence, is a supreme good. It should be the aim of education to make certain that in each period of his life the child is free to reach his fullest possible growth and maturity.

According to Rousseau there should be no concern about

prolonging the period of childhood, for such a course is far preferable to pushing the child ahead too fast toward adult maturity. The teacher should especially guard against premature stimulation of sexual feelings and other emotions more suitable for later stages of development. The child should be guided away from those mental images and fantasies which are more appropriate to adults. These images and fantasies had best be deferred to the period of adolescence, a time when his own discretion and rational powers will assist him in making judicious decisions. This injunction seems inconsistent with Rousseau's advocacy of negative education and the free play of natural impulses, and is undoubtedly a reflection of his own adolescent experiences. He thoroughly misunderstood the relationship between mental images of early childhood and sexual drives. He blamed society for what he assumed to be a prevalent overdevelopment of the child's sexual interests and also for social arrangements preventing the marriage of young people just at the time of their sexual maturity. In both respects, he said, civilization collides with nature.

To solve this problem of conflict between sexual impulses and social restrictions, Rousseau suggested the remedy of *sublimation,* whereby sexual impulses are directed toward socially acceptable objectives, as, for example, manifestations of sympathy, magnanimity, and gentleness. These feelings, however, are appropriate to youth rather than to childhood. Freud's comparable theory of sublimation was thus anticipated by Rousseau, who added the practical conclusion that the awakened sex drives of the adolescent, which would not be allowed a sexual outlet, should be redirected toward desirable social activity so that he would tend to forget his own desires and become absorbed in another's sorrows and joys. Inasmuch as self-love finds its counterpart in sympathy, sexual gratification, which provides satisfaction for the self, should similarly find its logical counterpart in sympathetic expression. Rousseau's objective was twofold; to enable the adolescent to control his sexual drives and at the same time to cultivate within himself sympathy for other human beings. Thus, in this circuitous manner, by means of sublimation, sexual impulses are ennobled; irrational instincts are transformed into wholesome emotions serving mankind. Out of sex, love blossoms.

Each period of life (infancy, childhood, adolescence, youth, and adulthood) is an independent one with its own goals, but continuity from one period to the next, as from childhood to adolescence, should be preserved. Later periods, said Rousseau, should not counteract but rather reinforce and carry forward the preceding ones.

IX *Man's Priceless Possession, Liberty*

Liberty, a precious gift, is necessary for the moral life. Although the faculty of reason distinguishes man from brute, reason can be regarded as worthy only of derision unless it is accompanied by freedom. There would be no difference between man and other animals if he failed to use his ability to think, if he always did whatever he was forced to do, if he acted under compulsion without reflection. Only the human being can deliberate, weigh and consider alternatives, and choose from among hundreds of ideas and courses of action. His freedom to make such rational choices, which sets him apart from the brute, gives the activity of reasoning value and significance.

Liberty implies imperfection, for beings already perfect would not need the freedom to seek perfection. Liberty to seek perfection, however, also implies freedom to choose corruption. Rather than being absolute, liberty changes and develops with every human advance. Consequently it does not mean the same thing to a savage as it does to a Socrates. As a human being grows to maturity, his freedom, which at the start was comparable to that of the wild beasts, changes radically because he learns to acknowledge duties, assume responsibilities, and faithfully observe allegiances. Doing whatever one pleases is a sign of irresponsibility, a pitiful condition, a brutal state in which one's slavery to appetite matches the gluttony of a savage. "Your freedom and your power extend as far and no farther than your natural strength; anything more is but slavery, deceit, and trickery."[22]

Rugged individualism, stoical independence, and the ability to live in solitude were prized by Rousseau, who felt that education should develop in the child these qualities of personality. "There is only one man who gets his own way—he who can get it singlehanded; therefore freedom, not power, is the greatest good. That man is truly free who desires what he is able to perform, and does what he desires. This is my fundamental maxim. Apply it to childhood, and all the rules of education spring from it."[23] Note the assumption that freedom is more precious than power.

Freedom, however, is not to be confused with license, for licentiousness is the path to misery. "Do you know the surest way to make your child miserable? Let him have everything he wants; for as his wants increase in proportion to the ease with which they are satisfied, you will be compelled, sooner or later, to refuse his demands, and this unlooked-for refusal will hurt him more than the lack of what he wants. He will want your stick first, then your watch, the bird that flies, or the star that shines above him. He will want all he sets eyes on, and unless you were God himself, how could you satisfy him?"[24] Excessive prosperity, according to Rousseau, is morally corrupting.

Freedom is an inalienable right. "Even if each man could alienate himself, he could not alienate his children: they are born men and free; their liberty belongs to them."[25] Liberty is a *sine qua non* of humanity; hence to divest oneself of it would make one inhuman. "To renounce liberty is to renounce being a man, to surrender the rights of humanity and even its duties."[26] One's liberty is precious and must be protected and guarded, for "liberty may be won, but can never be recovered."[27]

CHAPTER 3

Prolegomena to Education according to Nature

Rousseau's exhortation, "Back to the state of nature," based on the premise that "man is naturally good," is not a summons to replace civilization with savagery. Nor is his advocacy of education according to nature an invitation to transform the child into a primitive human being. He did not condemn all society as such, but only the artificial type of civilization of his time, which he blamed for man's deterioration. He argued for a new form of education of citizens as individuals in a more natural kind of society. He emphasized education of the individual in isolation, it is true, but only because the institutions and customs of his contemporary society had become evil influences upon children and adults alike. If they were properly educated, citizens would create a more democratic state adhering to high principles of morality, liberty, and justice.

I *Education for Citizenship*

The foundation stone of the new society for which citizens would be educated was Rousseau's classic doctrine of the *general will*. He set forth this doctrine in his article, "Political Economy," in the French *Encyclopedia* of 1755. He defined the "body politic" as a "moral being endowed with a

42

will." This doctrine of the general will has significance for the philosophy of education because a certain type of education is specified for any state in which the general will reigns supreme.

Furthermore Rousseau's article enunciated a socialist orientation to education in a relatively recent period. Education, in his view, is a governmental concern because fathers and families perish while the state endures; hence the state should oversee the education of its young. Moreover, education left to parents is subject to parental ignorance and prejudice. "The matter is one that concerns the state more than the fathers; for, in the course of nature, the death of the father often robs him of the final fruits of this education, but sooner or later the nation feels the effect of it. The state abides: the family passes."[1] The shift from parental tutelage to the performance of educational duties by the state is merely a nominal change, for the objectives remain the same. What occurs is simply that the people as a whole control education instead of allowing paternal control by individuals to continue unchecked. Each person realizes that he must obey the requirements imposed upon him by the law, just as he must abide by the laws of nature. Public education, a fundamental requirement of popular government, must conform to prescribed governmental regulations, subject to direction by duly appointed magistrates representing the supreme authority. In this manner, children will receive the same education and all will be on an equal footing, learning about state laws and acquiring respect for the general will. They will readily develop respect for the laws and the general will because they will be learning in an appropriate social atmosphere and environment, and since they will have teachers serving as models of loyal citizens, thus constantly reminding them "of the tender mother that fosters them, of the love she bears them, of the inestimable benefits they receive from her, and of the return they owe her, it cannot be doubted that they will learn in this way to cherish each other as brothers and wish only what the community wishes, and that one day they will become the defenders and the fathers of the country of which they have so long been the children."[2] It is the duty of government to select most carefully the magistrates to whom the education of children is to be entrusted. Unless the government performs this duty scrupulously, the system of education, which is the most important business of government and requires public confidence, will be ineffectual.

A lesson that lacks approval by authority, and a precept that is not reinforced by example, will render instruction futile. Virtue proclaimed by a teacher who fails to practice it is discredited. Accordingly, courage should be taught by brave military leaders and justice by experienced judges. Thus the task of instruction should be entrusted to individuals successful in life, not to teachers whose lives have been restricted to the classroom. Effective teachers are educated men who will become in their turn competent teachers, thereby providing successive generations with leadership representing the best experience, talent, courage, and virtue in the nation. Such education excites "universal emulation in all to live and die for their country." Rousseau maintained that it was this mode of education that was practiced successfully in ancient times among the Cretans, Spartans, and Persians.

One major difficulty inherent in this aspect of Rousseau's philosophy of education is the fact that nations have become extremely large and complex societies almost impossible to govern well. This difficulty was not so great in the eighteenth century as it is today, but even then his proposals would have encountered obstacles in practice, and no modern state has attempted to implement all or most of them. The ancient Romans, though never utilizing such procedures, reflected some of his basic educational objectives, inspiring the people with a hatred of tyranny, making their homes into schools of citizenship, and providing parental supervision of children so effective that they respected their father's commands even more than those of a magistrate. The Roman father, in his domestic domain, reinforced the validity of the laws and censored the morals of the young.

Rousseau held that education is the best means of insuring high standards of ethical conduct. Immorality flourishes because too many citizens are indifferent to the well-being of the nation as a whole and, therefore, children should be taught simultaneously moral behavior and love of country. Individuals should be taught not to indulge in excessive gratifications and self-aggrandizement which can only weaken the power and authority of the state. Little is required for the happiness of a people who possess good will, love their country, respect its laws, and pursue the simple life. A well-managed state which carefully plans its educational programs, leaving little to chance, enjoys the combined fruits of wisdom and happiness.

In a republic, education should be provided at an early age, for "a man should learn to deserve his life from the first instant of it; and, since he shares in civic rights as soon as he is born, the moment of birth ought to be the beginning of the performance of his duties."[3] Just as laws are necessary for adults, so there should be rules and regulations for children in order to teach them obedience.

Rousseau stressed the need for teaching morality because without it liberty will perish, and without liberty no true nation can exist. "Train up good citizens and you get everything," he said, else all citizens, from the lowliest subject to the rulers of the state, will be ignoble slaves. Education in citizenship must begin during infancy to be effective. Each human being must be educated to the very limits of his potential development. Such an education calls for the fullest expression and cultivation of his emotions, not their blockage or destruction. Moreover, elimination of the passions is altogether impossible, and, if it were possible, a passionless person would be a most undesirable citizen. The child should be taught appreciation of what is beautiful in preference to what is ugly or offensive in his surroundings. He should learn about his proper role as a citizen in the fatherland, a most important aspect of his education which should begin at an early age, teaching him to subordinate his self-interest as an individual to the well-being of the state as a whole, and inculcating in him the conviction that one's life is futile and meaningless except in so far as it derives from and is joined with that of the nation. By means of such education provided over an extended period of time, the individual will eventually acquire a sense of identification with the "grand Whole," that is, the state.

In effective education for citizenship, the individual will learn a point of view and philosophy which will point the way to new constructive emotional outlets, and these lessons will be supplemented by the study of historical personalities. Owing to the lack of interest in citizenship, too few dedicated leaders are to be found. Suitable means of teaching these lessons of citizenship during the early years of childhood have been neglected, a most deplorable deficiency since it is difficult to change undesirable fixed habits later in life, and it is virtually impossible when the individual's selfish habits have been reinforced by self-pride. Rousseau asserts that irreparable damage has been done by the time the individual becomes an adult with selfish aims and habits and petty ambitions dominating his personality. The miseducated adult, swayed by undesirable passions of avarice, lust, and vanity, which negate and stifle any love of country, no longer feels himself to be an integral part of his fatherland, a loyal citizen "loving it with the exquisite sentiment that the solitary man keeps for himself."

II *A National System of Education*

In his *Considerations on the Government of Poland and on Its Proposed Reformation* (published in 1772), Rousseau expounded an educational philosophy appropriate to any free state. He believed that only free men can derive proper benefits from education, which he viewed as a means of providing "souls a national formation," developing citizens whose beliefs, emotions, loyalties, and inclinations are inevitably patriotic. The type of education that would produce such results is suitable for a truly republican state in which law and liberty prevail, thereby contributing to a love of existence. For free men, meaningful life would cease without a fatherland to bind them together in a community governed by the rule of law. The wrong kind of society and education, however, can afflict men of any nationality. "A Frenchman, an Englishman, a Spaniard, an Italian, a Russian are all practically the same man; each leaves school already fully prepared for license, that is to say, for slavery."[4] The government of a free society should carefully plan programs of civic education befitting that society.

Thus, in learning to read, the child should read about his own land. The ten-year-old should become familiar with the products of his own country; at fifteen the pupil should know well its geography, including roads, towns, and provinces; at sixteen he should understand its laws. All pupils should study the careers of famous citizens and national leaders.

In Rousseau's proposed national system of education, priests and foreigners would be ineligible for teaching positions. Teachers would be married citizens of high moral character, successful experience, and endowed with practical common sense. "Beware above all of turning teaching into a profession. No public man...should have any other permanent rank than that of citizen."[5] Teachers are to be assigned on a trial basis, their positions being viewed as "testing-places" only, as steps on the ladder of advancement for meritorious appointees.

The constitution in Rousseau's republican state stipulates the equality of all citizens, a fundamental principle which forbids special privileges or distinctions, such as separate educational facilities for wealthy people. Free public education for all classes of citizens is the ideal system, but if tuition fees are unavoidable, the amount charged should be within the means of the poor, among whom the most deserving children should be given scholarships. The holders of scholarships should be known as "children of the state" entitled to wear "honorific insignia" as marks of distinction setting them apart from other children irrespective of economic status.

In this system of national education, physical health and vigor are essential objectives for the attainment of which every school should be equipped with a gymnasium or equivalent facility. Physical exercises and games should be assigned for the purpose of developing "robust and healthy physiques, but even more for moral purposes." Such provisions for free expression and movement, for natural development, are consistent with Rousseau's insistence that "good education ought to be negative. Prevent vices from arising, and you will have done enough for virtue."[6] Public education should be keynoted by *simplicity*. Boring studies beyond the child's comprehension should be avoided, and his hatred of the subject will increase when he is forced to remain seated, motionless, silent. "Children," he said, "are always moving about. Sedentary life is harmful." Body exercises and games, with their attendant pleasure, contribute greatly to the achievement of wholesome growth in an atmosphere of self-direction and spontaneity.

But self-direction, according to Rousseau, is not incompatible with a most essential process of socialization of the individual. The child should play with other children, never alone, for he must learn to share with them a common goal, competing with and emulating the best of his companions. Even parents who prefer to educate their children in the home should nevertheless arrange for their children to participate in these public games and exercises which should be open to all. Games involve more than agility and muscular development; they teach the lessons of equality, fraternity, and fair competition, an appreciation for rules, and the right kind of response to public approbation. Prizes and awards, which have salutary effects, should be presented attractively in public ceremonies.

Rousseau expressed astonishment at the fact that his numerous ideas on education, which to him appeared both beneficial and practical, were never implemented. It seemed to him that nothing could be more important than the abandonment of outworn shibboleths of corrupted institutions and the eradication of the poisonous egoistic philosophy of education then in vogue, so that a new nation could emerge. It is not surprising, therefore, that he seized upon the opportunity to expound the preceding views concerning a national program of education when a Polish patriot, just before the first dismemberment of his country by Prussia and Russia, asked for them. Rousseau hoped that his educational ideas stated in the treatise of 1772 might at last be implemented, a futile prospect since Poland was soon to be repeatedly partitioned. Although his ideas on education dealt with much more than the training of citizens, his treatise contended that only in an ideal state is the finest education possible.

III *Education of a Bored Child*

John Locke's ideas on the importance of educating youth (in his essay, *Some Thoughts concerning Education,* published in 1693) impelled Rousseau to embark upon a teaching career, but, after teaching two recalcitrant boys for about a year, he found himself to be temperamentally unfit for such an occupation. His *modus operandi* for training the two boys (sons of M. de Malby, provost of Lyon) was described in 1740 in his treatise, *Project for the Education of M. de Sainte-Marie,* written after seven or eight months of teaching. The boys Sainte-Marie and Condillac were nephews of the distinguished philosopher Condillac whom Rousseau highly esteemed. Rousseau was then only twenty-eight years old.

In the report on his teaching methods, Rousseau condemned corporal punishment for misbehavior, one reason being that it ceases to have any effect as soon as the feeling of pain ends, and he recommended mental punishment instead because of the continuing effect. Thus, if a pupil fails to study his lessons, the appropriate punishment will be to deprive him of any and all forms of amusement until he completes the assignments. It is quite certain that, if the boy does not co-operate and yield gracefully to the requirements and is left out of enjoyable activities altogether, he will become perfectly bored, so weary of the futile situation that he will eventually be compelled to attend to his studies. In this way he will learn to appreciate the difference between idleness and honest work and understand that happy diversions or recreations are justifiable only as forms of relaxation after work, privileges not appropriate or necessary for idlers.

Rousseau advocated close co-operation between the child's father and the teacher in order to achieve effective educational results. The father should, for example, administer punishment or bestow rewards based upon the teacher's reports about the pupil's work. (Rousseau even described secret signals whereby the teacher can indicate the pupil's progress or lack of it so that the father can know whether to greet his son with approval and gifts.) The father should also question the child about academic studies, but mainly to ascertain positive achievements and thus encourage enthusiastic interest and continued effort. Occasionally, however, in case of ill-health or similar causes of retardation, sympathetic inquiry and display of concern may be helpful.

Discussing the proper relationship between the teacher and pupils such as the two recalcitrant boys he was teaching, Rousseau concluded that an admixture of affection and respect for the teacher should prevail. He had faith that the pupils would readily perceive that rewards and punishments were natural consequences of their behavior and accomplishments, not capricious or impulsive actions of the teacher or the parent. Accordingly, he suggested that teachers and parents should adhere to the following procedures: (1) parental rewards of the child should be given only after a favorable report and recommendation by the teacher; (2) the child's request for any favor or privilege directed to the parent should be referred to the teacher; and (3) the parent should make a reward or gift contingent upon good rapport between pupil and teacher. Furthermore, the child should be made aware of the advantages to be derived from a good education, as well as the disadvantages resulting from wasting time on useless or undesirable activities. In the end, however, the teacher represents authority and should utilize appropriate means to make certain that his pupil meets responsibilities. Of course, Rousseau did not regard the foregoing procedures as rigid, universally inviolable rules, but rather as suggestions amenable to modifications justified by circumstances.

In his treatise Rousseau expressed his steadfast conviction that "the education of a young man is to form his heart, his judgment, and his mind—in that order."[7] It was his view that, although acquisition of knowledge should not be neglected as an aim of education, the development of high moral character merits at least equal priority, especially in the case of a child endowed with keen intelligence and pliable personality. "What is the good of a man knowing Varro, if at the same time he has the misfortune to get his heart corrupted, if the knowledge in his head is like weapons in the hands of a madman? Of two people, equally immersed in vice, the one less educated will always do less evil."[8]

Moreover, ignorance and lack of education are preferable to knowledge accompanied by contempt for the truth.

Religion and morality cannot be taught effectively like a multiplication table by means of drill or memorization of facts. Teacher and parent can inspire high standards of conduct which will persist throughout life if they provide proper guidance of the child in his everyday experience whenever the opportunity for moral lessons arises. For education in ethical conduct, incidental learning, as in casual conversation, is more productive than formal prescribed courses of study because of the following advantages: (1) incidental learnings are not distasteful, as formal lessons too often are; (2) moral questions involving actual experience require the child to form habits of careful reflection about cause-and-effect relationships; and (3) situations requiring moral decisions stimulate the child's curiosity and challenge his powers.

"Integrity of heart," said Rousseau, "when fortified by reason produces an accurate mind."[9] Almost invariably a good man thinks accurately, and buttressed with some experience he will possess the necessary requisites for forming good judgments. Good judgments are contingent more on the heart's fine sentiments than on mental ability, as is evidenced by the fact that educated and enlightened persons are not necessarily those who best conduct themselves in the business of life. Conversely, people who observe high moral standards in their daily lives demonstrate thereby their excellent intelligence. Pupils can be taught to observe others carefully and from their guided experience acquire understanding of the psychology motivating human beings, thus becoming able to see people as they really are, in all their virtues and vices, and to make wise choices when faced with life's problems or vicissitudes.

Consequently, the pupil should be in the company of other people and acquire ease and facility in communicating with them. For this purpose, practical experience in the world of work and in everyday affairs is essential. Parents can easily arrange for such experience, perhaps as a form of reward or recreation; they can, for example, take the children along on

a visit or on business, or have the children present when
guests are being entertained in the home. From such experiences a child can develop poise and self-confidence, especially
if he is permitted to participate in the conversation of adults.
If the parent guides these experiences so that they will be
suitable in view of the child's age, more knowledge of the
world will be gained in a few hours than could be acquired
in a year of formal class instruction.

Knowledge is always both good and useful. Pedantry, however, is attributable to a bad disposition. True men of learning are both refined and modest; their genuine understanding protects them from vanity. Only men with imperfect
knowledge, pretending to know all, assume a supercilious
air. Educated men know that one of life's greatest resources
is a well developed interest in reading, for books always provide a source of pleasure. One's library is his refuge from the
world. "There are so many unjust deeds done in the world
and so many changes of fortune, that a man has often occasion to count himself happy that he can find friends and
comforters in his library to compensate for those whom the
world takes from him or refuses to him."[10]

IV *Indebtedness to John Locke*

It was the great philosopher Hegel who pointed out that
no one develops his thinking in a vacuum, but constructs his
ideas upon foundations laid by others. In the case of Rousseau, he was heavily indebted to Hobbes (1588-1679) and
Locke (1632-1704) for the springboard of his political ideas,
and he was chiefly indebted to Locke's *Some Thoughts concerning Education* (1693) for many of his views on education.

In the seventeenth century the philosophy of education
dominant during the late Middle Ages (1300-1500), with its
theological foundations, reflected in the assumption that
man is born depraved and fallen and must strive to attain a
new divine state, was beginning to give way to a different
point of view well stated by John Locke in the work cited
above: "That a Man is to...purely follow what Reason directs as best, tho' the Appetite lean the other Way." Physical
and mental discipline, as in the use of body exercises and the

study of mathematics and other subjects supplements religious training. Locke held that the mind of a person at birth is a *tabula rasa* (blank tablet or white paper) which receives indelible impressions from the senses throughout life. The mind develops its powers by reflecting upon these experiences with logical reasoning. Locke's fundamental thesis, set forth in his *An Essay concerning Human Understanding*, a book which in 1690 marked the opening of the period of the Enlightenment, is stated as follows:

Let us then suppose the mind to be, as we say, white paper, void of all characters, without any *ideas*. How comes it to be furnished? Whence comes it by that vast store, which the busy and boundless fancy of man has painted on it with an almost endless variety? To this I answer, in one word, from *experience; in that all our knowledge is founded, and from that it ultimately derives itself. Our observation, employed either about *external, sensible objects, or about the internal operations of our minds, perceived and reflected on by ourselves, is that which supplies our understandings with all the materials of thinking.* These two are the fountains of knowledge, from whence all the *ideas* we have, or can naturally have, do spring.[11]

Locke's view undoubtedly influenced Rousseau, even though the latter's insistence upon free activity in conformity with nature differs from the former's advocacy of logical presentation of subject matter. Rousseau agreed enthusiastically, however, with Locke's assertion in *Of Civil Government* that men are born free, equal, and independent.

Holding steadfast to his conviction that man's natural powers are good, that he is born good, Rousseau repudiated the doctrine of original sin. He believed that society is artificial and corrupt, but that the individuals in society are naturally good until they are corrupted by society. He rejected the practice of teaching Christian morality by means of catechetical memoriter lessons about original sin and pleaded for the development of the child's natural good impulses by rational choices based on "evidence and demonstration," following Locke's view that *"reason is natural revelation,"* God's chosen technique for man's discovery of truth. Locke equated revelation and reason, asserting that "*revelation* is natural *reason* enlarged by a new set of discoveries communicated by God immediately, which reason vouches the truth of, by the testimony and proofs it gives that they come from God. So that he that takes away *reason*, to make way for *revelation*, puts out the light of both."[12]

Rousseau was indebted to Locke not only for these concepts of empiricism elaborated in his *Essay concerning Human Understanding*, but also for specific educational theories and practical suggestions set forth in Locke's *Some Thought concerning Education*, and Rousseau articulated many such ideas in his *Project for the Education of M. de Sainte-Marie*. Rousseau's analysis of the common misuse of punishment for misbehavior, for example, echoes Locke's observation that corporal punishment has mainly the effect of convincing the child that education is a painful bore to be avoided. Rousseau agreed with Locke that education should be an enjoyable experience, that physical pain from whipping "only patches up for the present, and skims it over, but reaches not to the bottom of the sore; ingenuous *shame,* and the apprehensions of displeasure, are the only true restraint."[13]

Rousseau accepted Locke's admonition that "children are *not* to be *taught by rules* which will be always slipping out of their memories. What you think necessary for them to do, settle in them by an indispensable practice, as often as the occasion returns; and if it be possible, make occasions."[14] Learning through repetitive experience and practice is far superior to mere memorization.

Locke held that children learn by imitating respected adults, such as their parents or friends, and Rousseau reiterated the same conclusion. "You will have very good luck, if you never have a clownish or vicious servant, and if from them your children never get any infection: But yet as much must be done towards it as can be, and the children kept as much as may be in *the company of their parents,* and those to whose care they are committed. To this purpose, their being in their presence should be made easy to them."[15] Rousseau recommended that parents, not teachers, should bestow rewards upon children. "To make them in love with the *company of their parents,* they should receive all their good things there, and from their hands."[16]

Interest and enthusiastic effort, said Locke, are essential, and the proper approach to teaching is to give children "a liking and inclination to what you propose to them to be learn'd, and that will engage their industry and application."[17] Rousseau made use of this idea, as well as Locke's suggestion that when a child "can talk, 'tis time he should begin to *learn to read.* ... I have always had a fancy that *learning* might be made a play and recreation to children; and that they might be brought to desire to be taught, if it were proposed to them as a thing of honour, credit, delight, and recreation."[18] Locke added that children can "be taught to read, without perceiving it to be anything but a sport." Rousseau popularized Locke's related view that the love of liberty must be developed from "our cradles" onward, that men should be and feel free to direct their own conduct.

Locke pointed out that good relationships between parents and teachers are necessary for successful teaching. Parents should respect teachers, and should encourage others to do so, in order that teachers may sustain their authority and influence among pupils. "You cannot expect your son should have any regard for one whom he sees you, or his mother, or others slight." One should not retain a teacher whom he holds in contempt, for the contagion of this negative attitude will infect the pupil.

Locke's observation that a teacher must teach by example as well as by precept also impressed Rousseau. "As the father's example must teach the child respect for his tutor, so the tutor's example must lead the child into those actions he would have him do. His practice must by no means cross his precepts, unless he intend to set him wrong."[19]

Rousseau's famous principle that the child should be educated, not by books or artificial set tasks, but by the book of nature, by natural experience and activities, is similar to Locke's idea that children should be taught by repeated practice, continuous action under the trained watchful eye of the tutor and under his direction so that only the pupil's natural habits will be developed and the unnatural ones will be nipped in the bud. "By this method we shall see whether what is required of him be adapted to his capacity, and any way suited to the child's natural genius and constitution; for that too must be considered in a right education. We must not hope wholly to change their original tempers, nor make the gay pensive and grave, nor the melancholy sportive, without spoiling them. God has stamped certain characters upon men's minds, which like their shapes, may perhaps be a little mended, but can hardly be totally altered and transformed into the contrary."[20] Much is made of this point in Rousseau's educational writings.

Rousseau's admonition about the moral factor, its importance and its place in education, was also anticipated by Locke, who commented: "He therefore that is about children should well study their natures and aptitudes, and see by often trails what turn they easily take, and what becomes them; observe what their native stock is, how it may be improved, and what it is fit for: He should consider what they want, whether they be capable of having it wrought into them by industry, and incorporated there by practice; and whether it be worth while to endeavor it. For in many cases, all that we can do, or should aim at, is, to make the best of what nature has given, to prevent the vices and faults to which such a constitution is most inclined, and give it all the advantages it is capable of. Every one's natural genius should be carried as far as it could."[21] Care should be taken lest another's personality, one foreign to his disposition, be imposed upon the child.

The foregoing ideas of Locke on education made up a great part of Rousseau's early thinking and, in fact, dominated educational philosophy until the mid-nineteenth century. Rousseau later supplemented these concepts after considering the views of Montaigne, Fénelon, and the French Encyclopedists, to all of which he contributed his own unique emphases, as in the insistence that education should counteract the evil institutions and customs of society.

V Education During Rousseau's Lifetime

The philosophy of John Locke helped give birth to the Enlightenment, which rejected medieval reliance upon authority and urged men to act as free minds searching for truth by means of scientific investigation and logical reasoning. Locke's *An Essay concerning Human Understanding* expressed what was to become the modern point of view that sense experience and reason constitute the best possible sources of knowledge. In his *Some Thoughts concerning Education,* Locke presented similar views on education, accepted wholeheartedly by Rousseau who held that children must be treated as persons entitled to respect and status as human beings capable of self-direction and free self-development. Medieval people had regarded children as miniature adults or as impulsive little animals to be treated almost as if they were toys, clothed like adults, carrying on activities that were crude imitations of adult games and sexual interests. Most parents devoted little attention to children, and most children, as well as adults, were illiterate. Often children had no significance for adults except as a source of economic values or legal bonds. Medieval educators with few exceptions had only a vague appreciation of child development.

An attitude belittling children, perhaps attributable in part to their low life expectancy, seems to have remained common, even at times afflicting respectable and distinguished intellects such as Rousseau and Montaigne. Rousseau, without much remorse prior to his *The Confessions,* claimed that he had abandoned his five illegitimate children to orphanages. Montaigne casually remarked that he had lost two or three offspring in their infancy and then added, "not without regret, but without great grief."

The psychology of adolescence was then practically unknown. "People had no idea of what we call adolescence, and the idea was a long time taking shape. . . . Society has passed from a period which was ignorant of adolescence to a period in which adolescence is the favourite age."[22] Just as adolescence is the privileged age of the twentieth century, youth was that of the seventeenth and eighteenth centuries. Old age was looked upon with contempt.

During the late seventeenth and early eighteenth centuries the attitude toward children began to change. Many no longer dressed as adults, but wore clothing reserved for

their particular age group. After the French Revolution, the
trousers worn by boys, adapted from the military uniforms,
became acceptable court dress. Before the seventeenth century, only infants were expected to take part in games, but
thereafter children played adult-type games either with
adults or with their peers. Eventually the period of childhood
was commonly depicted as the age of innocence, toward
which there were two widespread attitudes: (1) a protective
attitude expressed in efforts to protect children from sexual
temptations and corruption by life experience; and (2) a
practical, rational attitude expressed in efforts to reinforce
the natural impulses of children by means of character education and intellectual training. "The association of childhood with primitivism and irrationalism or prelogicism
characterizes our contemporary concept of childhood. This
concept made its appearance in Rousseau, but it belongs to
twentieth-century history."[23] The view that innocent emotional impulses conflict with disciplined reason was not accepted by the people of Rousseau's time, as it seems to have
been in the twentieth century. Between the seventeenth century and the late nineteenth century, the most vivid man-
ifestation of this view of childhood was to be seen in the
First Holy Communion ceremony, portraying both the child's
innocence or purity and his rational comprehension of the
mysteries of religion.

The idea of childhood as a natural stage of continuous
human development was unknown to most people in medieval
and early modern times, for children were simply taken for
granted as appendages in the adult society, working as ap-
prentices or serving as pages to knights, and the like. Since
infants could not participate, they simply "did not count," as
Molière put it. Montaigne regarded the attention paid to
children as insufferable, referring to them as unlovable
owing to their lack of mental activity and recognizable bod-
ily shape; and he could not bring himself to love them "for
our amusement, like monkeys." The pedagogues in the
seventeenth century shared Montaigne's dislike for "coddling" children, a practice which was disappearing among the
upper classes and educated adults, and was being condemned
also by people in the lower classes before the turn of the

century. A treatise on education, *El Discreto* by Balthazar
Gratien, reminded readers about the "insipidity of childhood"
that "disgusts the sane mind." Childhood and youth were
looked upon as a disease that only time could cure.

In Rousseau's time progress was being made in elementary
education as parents and teachers began to understand the
process whereby the individual child slowly develops maturity in childhood and adolescence. Discipline was no longer a
simple matter of physical punishment and repressive control
but a means of instilling moral values, toughness, and viril-
ity. Adolescence was being differentiated from childhood as
such. The adolescent was expected to develop sturdy character and personality traits comparable to those of his counterpart, the soldier. Until the age of ten years, most children
who were to be educated were taught individually in the
home; thereafter they enrolled in small classes of ten or
fewer pupils, as in the typical schools of Sainte-Barbe and
those at Port-Royal.

In France during the late eighteenth and early nineteenth
centuries, the kind of private instruction advocated by Rousseau, with children isolated from their families and society,
was regarded as a superior type of education. The boarding
school became an integral part of the French system. The
moral environment of the child was considered to be a
paramount consideration, as, for example, in the Jesuit
schools which provided around-the-clock supervision of
pupils. By the end of the eighteenth century Rousseau's view
that morality and education are enhanced by seclusion had
gained wide recognition. Some schools would not even allow
pupils to leave the premises on Sundays and holidays.

The boarding schools (including the elementary *licensed
schools* and the *little colleges*) had become popular in the
eighteenth century and catered to those parents who wanted
their children ten to fifteen years of age to live at small
schools in the country instead of crowded institutions with
constantly expanding enrollments. Eventually, in addition to
the licensed elementary schools and little colleges, a third
type of schools evolved which accepted students of all ages,
teaching the young ones until the fourth grade, but sending
the older pupils to study at the university while providing

them with supplementary tutelage. Many of the later colleges were only centers of class instruction and did not provide the lodging and moral supervision offered by the boarding schools.

Early in the eighteenth century the Jesuit schools, with their emphasis upon Latin, theological hair-splitting and medieval logic, harsh discipline, and frivolous memoriter learning, began to come into disrepute. In response to public criticism and demand for instruction in the Bible, arithmetic, history, geography, language, and various practical subjects, such as music and etiquette, "little schools" or grammar schools were organized throughout the country. The demands of the enlightened bourgeois were reinforced by the libertarian propaganda of great educators such as René de la Chalotais who, in his influential work, *Essay on National Education* (1763) agitated for education in citizenship and, of course, Rousseau whose *Emile* did much to change public attitudes toward childhood and the psychology of human development.

CHAPTER 4

Julie, or the New Heloise

Although Rousseau's *Julie, or the New Heloise* is not a great novel so far as skillful construction is concerned, it is, like his most famous *Emile,* unexcelled as a morality novel. In fact, both works may be regarded as treatises rather than as novels, though the narrative thread is maintained throughout in each. The plot in *Julie, or the New Heloise* is mainly autobiographical, patterned to some extent after Samuel Richardson's epistolary novel *Clarissa, or the History of a Young Lady.* (Rousseau's novel was subtitled *Letters of Two Lovers, Inhabitants of a Small Village at the Foot of the Alps, Collected and Published, &c.*)

Rousseau's books met with sharp reactions: *Julie, or the New Heloise* was branded as immoral; the sentimental deism elaborated in the "Profession of the Vicar of Savoy" contained in *Emile* offended both the church and the *philosophe* party; and *The Social Contract* was considered antimonarchistic. A novel constructed with a number of written letters, *Julie, or the New Heloise* depicts the love of a man of the lower class for a girl of a higher class, describing the agonies of the lover, the way in which the suffering of the lovers is meliorated by the intervention of a humanitarian Englishman, and the eventual marriage of the girl to a freethinker of her own class in society.

Rousseau wrote most of the *New Heloise,* as it is often called, in the late 1750's when he was a seasoned thinker of middle age. At that time he lived in Montmorency where he enjoyed solitude, wandering in the forests, reflecting and communing with the divine, recovering from an illness in the mild country environment. His religion was that of the world, the worship of a solitary free man, a worship of the Deity rooted in all that was natural in his surroundings. Despite vexatious quarrels with friends and the consequent moral turmoil that plagued him in the winter of 1758, Rousseau persisted in his writing and soon completed the *New Heloise* and *Emile*. The former novel was probably finished in 1759, and it was published in 1761; the great classic *Emile* appeared a year later. Both works were acclaimed widely and enjoyed resounding success, which seemed to prove he had chosen the right vocation for himself. But he did not believe such a choice would necessarily work out well for other people, and when a young man considering a similar intellectual vocation consulted him, Rousseau sent him off with the comment: "The first lesson I should give you would be not to surrender yourself to the taste you say you have for the contemplative life, which is only an indolence of the soul, to be condemned at any age, but especially at yours. Man is not made to meditate but to act."[1] He advised the youth to seek some occupation that would be approved by God and family as a significant and virtuous endeavor.

I *Central Theme of the Novel*

The book centers around Julie, an unsophisticated girl who, since her heart is her compass, feels that she needs no other guide, not even reason. She lives with complete devotion to love and utter disregard for consequences. She becomes the mistress of her tutor Saint-Preux, a man she had loved but had renounced out of obedience to her parents who looked down upon him as a man endowed with meager assets and unlikely to rise above his middle-class status. Rather than offend her parents, especially her mother who was seriously ill, Julie yields to parental authority, allows her lover to depart, and marries M. de Wolmar, her father's choice.

Rousseau defended in this novel the right of the pure in

heart to love sincerely—a right basic to the sanctity of marriage and family relationships—in a society which hypocritically treated an honest but impulsively indiscreet woman with disgrace and contempt while it winked at widespread infidelity. He portrayed Julie as a devoted daughter who obeys the wishes of her parents and the marriage customs of society, yet, like Heloise the lady love of the great medieval philosopher Abelard, fulfills the role of a new Heloise and loves Saint-Preux contrary to her marriage vows. The story highlights the conflict between Julie's submissiveness and her right to full self-expression and personal freedom.

Discussing the dilemma of this central theme, Rousseau seized the opportunity to expound his views on religion and education. He set forth his religious beliefs in the form of a dialogue between two highly respected persons, one a freethinker, the other an atheist, his main purpose being to narrow the gap between the freethinking Encyclopedists and people adhering to theism.

II *A Philosophy of Life*

Rousseau's preoccupation with profound religious concepts led him into self-reflection and, consequently, his moral commitments. Reviewing the errors of his youth, he set himself the task of delineating the correct path of education, especially the proper ethical aims to be fulfilled. He expressed moral convictions concerning all aspects of education as it affects individuals, the family, and other social institutions. He could not keep silent about the drastic social and educational reforms needed, nor restrain reiteration of his explosive ideas elaborated in the *New Heloise* consisting of nearly one hundred fifty epistolary exchanges among the main characters—Julie, Wolmar, Saint-Preux, and Milord Edward—concerning education, morality, and religion.

In one of these letters, an autobiographical letter from Lord Bomton, Rousseau discussed the youthful missteps he had made owing to his zeal for successful achievement. The mature person, he asserted, no longer considers it important to devote himself to ambitious accomplishments and rewards. "At thirty years of age surely a man should begin to reflect. Reflect, therefore, and be a man, at least once before you die."[2] He lamented the fact that young people allow their feelings to hold sway over and pervert their understanding, so that their immaturity prevents them from formulating a rational, logically consistent philosophy of life. They make a fundamental error in confusing feeling for rational judgment. Rousseau expressed this criticism succinctly: "Your heart, my dear friend, has long imposed on your understanding. You strove to philosophize before you were capable of it, mistaking your feelings for reason."[3] Yet, since feeling has its important role to play, he went on to say: "A good heart, I will own, is indispensably necessary to the knowledge of truth: he who feels nothing can learn nothing."[4] Thus Rousseau agreed with Blaise Pascal that the heart has its reasons which the mind does not know, but he also pointed out that one must learn self-control so that the soul will conquer passions and live according to law and moral values.

Having enjoyed life, "the only object of contemplation should be yourself."[5] He who has at one time been enslaved by his passions is fortunate if he is not deprived of his virtue. "There is no such thing as virtue without fortitude, for pusillanimity is the certain attendant on vice."[6] The most that one can derive from interpersonal relationships is aid in determining the correct course to pursue.

III *Education through Self-direction*

One of the letters in the *New Heloise* which describes the education of Julie's two children constitutes a most concise and well-rounded statement of Rousseau's philosophy of education. The letter pertains to the family of Julie, then the wife of M. de Wolmar, and is written by Saint-Preux, Julie's former lover and currently an honored guest in Wolmar's home.

As was their custom, the children came to Julie's room following breakfast. Instead of shutting herself off from the children and confining them to their room, Julie permitted them to remain with her. The two boys were learning their lessons without strained effort or constraint while perusing a

collection of pictures; as they leafed through the pictures, the older boy explained them to the younger one, and no one interfered or interrupted except occasionally to correct an error which might be overheard.

Julie remained close to her children throughout the days, but never entered into disputes with them, nor did she forbid any of their activities. Like other boys of their age level, they were full of energy, busy with all sorts of projects, but keeping everything within reasonable bounds. "They are already discreet, before they know what discretion is."[7] Their sense of discretion developed naturally in the well-managed family. If controversy between the two boys arose, the mother did not attempt to pacify either of them, and they learned to imitate her sensible attitudes and rational conduct. When the boys turned to piling counters in a row and the younger one became inattentive, the older boy scattered them on the floor in anger, but the younger child was allowed to cry without efforts to pacify him, yet later, after the counters had been removed altogether, he did not have recourse to tears or regrets. Thus in this well-managed family, difficulties caused by the children were kept at a minimum. "I should willingly have attributed the goodness of the children to the mother. I thought it would have been better if they owed less to nature and more to the mother, and I could almost have desired some faults in them that I might have seen her more solicitous to correct them."[8]

A virtuous mother's qualities are transmitted to her children. "Heaven rewards the virtue of mothers in the good disposition of their children."[9] The writer of this letter, Saint-Preux, continued, quoting his remarks to Julie and her replies: " 'but this good disposition needs to be cultivated. Their education ought to commence with birth. Is there a time more suited to form their minds than when they have received no impression that need be effaced? If you let them have their own way in childhood, at what age do you expect them to be docile? Even if you had nothing else to teach them, you ought to teach them obedience.' 'Have you,' she replied, 'seen my children disobeying me?' 'That would be difficult,' said I, 'since you impose no commands upon them.' "[10]

IV Readiness for Learning

Julie proceeded to expound her philosophy of education. Although she had seemed to neglect the children, she was in fact always devoting vigilant attention to them as an expression of her maternal love. "The first and most important part of education, precisely that which all the world neglects, is that of preparing a child to receive instruction."[11] Even Locke failed to understand this basic principle of readiness, for "he taught concerning the things that one ought to require of his child instead of the means of obtaining them."[12] Many parents who pride themselves on their own knowledge and intelligence erroneously assume that their child's ability to reason logically is innate, inherited from them. Consequently they speak to their children (even before they have learned to talk) as if they were adults. They take it for granted that the power to reason logically makes learning possible, that other faculties are ancillary to reason. Of all the capacities that mankind requires, however, the last to be acquired, and the one attained with the greatest difficulty, is reason. By speaking to very young children in a language they do not understand, one teaches them to be satisfied with mere words, often contradicting everything that is said. They fancy themselves as wise as their teachers, cultivating an argumentative spirit and rebellious attitude. Although one may sometimes seem to be motivating children's achievements by appealing to their reason, the really effective forces are their ulterior motives, such as fear and vanity, which necessarily affect their response to such an appeal.

The verbalistic method of education taxes the patience of the most tolerant of parents, who indeed become so exhausted thereby that they often shed their parental responsibilities and ship the children off to a schoolmaster, "as if one could expect to extract from a schoolteacher a patience, forbearance, and good-naturedness surpassing those of the child's own father." "Nature," said Julie, "would have children be children before they are men. If we attempt to pervert that order, we shall produce only premature fruit, which has neither maturity nor flavor, and will soon decay; we

shall have young professionals and aged children. Childhood has a manner of seeing, thinking, and feeling, peculiar to itself. Nothing can be more senseless than substituting our ways in its stead. I should as soon expect a youngster to be five feet tall, as to possess mature judgment at ten years of age."[13] Just as the body develops co-ordination and strength, so reason has its natural periods of development and maturity. Nature's design requires the body to develop prior to mental maturity. This is why children are constantly active; they are rarely idle, but move about in a lively way so that the body will develop well. The sedentary life of classroom study inhibits normal growth and development, inasmuch as neither the body nor the mind is able to endure habitual restraint. "Shut up perpetually in a room with their books, they lose their vigor, become delicate, feeble, sickly, and stupid rather than reasonable; and all throughout life the mind suffers owing to the weakness of the body."[14]

V *Individual Differences*

Even if one assumed that premature instruction conferred benefits equal to its disadvantages, it would still be inadvisable to give such education indiscriminately to children without taking into consideration what is most suitable for the genius of each child as an individual, because every child possesses his own individual qualities, a temperament of his own, as well as a constitution common to all human beings. "Besides a constitution common to the species, every child at its birth possesses a peculiar temperament, which determines its genius and character; and which it is improper either to pervert or to restrain; the business of education being only to provide a model and bring it to perfection."[15] Therefore education is properly not a process of altering or restraining natural propensities, but a process of developing them to perfection. The child's native character or initial equipment is in each case good and sound, for nature is unerring. "All of these characteristics are. . .good in themselves: For nature. . .makes no mistakes."[16] The vices ordinarily imputed to nature are actually attributable to the perversions induced by incorrect training. Accordingly "there is not a scoundrel on earth whose natural propensity, well directed, would not have been productive of great virtues."[17] Even the most distorted mind would develop useful qualities if it were given suitable direction and essential purposes. The same thing is true of figures or designs that seem ugly and deformed until one views them properly, and then they become beautiful and well-proportioned.

In education the proper approach is to do nothing because "in the universal system of nature, everything tends toward the common good,"[18] with each individual in his most suitable niche and the best possible order. Instead of disturbing or destroying nature's way, each person should learn to understand his own place in the order of things. Most effective will be that "system of education which begins in the cradle" to carry out the principle of educating according to nature and continues thereafter to implement that principle consistently. On the other hand, a system of education that disregards the vast diversity of temperaments, minds, and peculiar geniuses of individuals will result in the harmful, misdirected instruction of children, and the instruction called for which will best suit them will be woefully ignored. "Nature will be confined on every side, and the greatest qualities of the mind effaced, and mean, petty, unreal ones substituted in their place."[19]

The practice of assigning a great variety of programs uniformly to the same children, without considering their individual differences, will inevitably destroy some of their natural gifts while overemphasizing others, the net result being turmoil. "Thus, after considerable pains have been wasted in spoiling the natural endowments of children, we before long see those transitory and frivolous ones of education decay and vanish, while the natural ones, being totally eclipsed, no longer appear."[20] Consequently both the natural and the artificial potentialities of man are lost, for even that which man has created, he destroys. The consequences of such foolishly misspent effort will be that their little prodigies will grow up devoid of strength of character and mental acumen, and will become conspicuously useless and inefficient.

Saint-Preux inquired whether it would be preferable to

correct nature, that is, to structure a perfect model of a person, one who is upright and rational, and then strive to make every child comport as much as possible to the model through the vehicle of education so that the course of some children is accelerated while that of others is decelerated. Saint-Preux went on to inquire whether the mental powers and talents distinguishing one individual from another are actually the work of nature inasmuch as if nature were responsible for making people unequal, it could be accused of inequitable favoritism in endowing some individuals with keener intelligence, superior memories, and more acute senses and attentive abilities than others. If, however, mental diversity were not the work of nature but the product of education, then it would be necessary to ascertain the most desirable traits of character and proceed with dispatch to educate the children accordingly. Julie's husband replied to Saint-Preux that two dogs from the same litter with the same training and treatment may develop diametrically opposite temperaments so that one will be lively, affectionate, and intelligent, while the other will be surly, stupid, and incorrigible. "Only their difference in temperament can have produced the difference in character, just as the difference in our internal organization produces in us a difference in mental equipment. In every other circumstance they have been alike."[21] Saint-Preux raised the possibility that a number of minute, imperceptible factors could have had an effect on the situation. This objection was dismissed as the fallacy of pleading ignorance, with the analogy: "I find you reason like the astrologers, who, when two men are mentioned possessing different fortunes yet born under the same aspect of the stars, deny the aspect of the circumstances. On the contrary, they maintain that, on account of the rapidity of heavenly motions, there must have been an immense distance between the schemes of the men in the horoscope, and that if the precise instance of their births had been carefully noted, the objection would have been converted into proof."[22]

On careful observation it becomes evident that among some children outstanding characteristics are detectable almost at birth. These children, forming a class of their own, can be studied from infancy. Consequently their education may begin at birth. Among slowly developing children, however, since their special attributes cannot be immediately ascertained, wisdom dictates that education respecting the formation of their minds must be deferred until their distinctive bent becomes apparent, for otherwise there will be a high risk of spoiling nature's own handiwork and innate goodness by replacing it with something undesirable.

Plato was right in contending that education or any other art of man is incapable of extracting from the mind what was not initially there by nature, just as all the operations of chemistry are incapable of extracting more gold from a mixture than the amount which the mixture already contains. Although this limitation is not valid in regard to human sentiments and ideas, it does hold good for dispositions, the primitive elements that lead to their acquisition. "To change the mind, one must be able to alter its internal organization; to change a person's character, one must be capable of changing the temperament on which it depends. Have you ever heard of an emotional personality becoming phlegmatic, or a cold methodical mind acquiring an imaginative spirit?"[23] It is interesting to note that Rousseau has been advocating, and emphatically so at this point, a constitutional psychology along the lines developed by the distinguished German psychiatrist Ernst Kretschmer (1888-1964) and the contemporary American psychologist William H. Sheldon. Rousseau went on to argue that to transform a fool into a learned man is analogous to attempting to make a black man white. Any attempt to transform diverse minds into a single mold or common model would be futile. Constrain them as you will but to change them is impossible. The most that will be accomplished is that their real nature will be disguised, but their basic nature can never be altered. To succeed in camouflaging them means only that in time they will revert to their original characteristic nature when decisive circumstances arise. They will on such occasion revert with great abandon because of the sudden lifting of restraint. The task of education is not to alter or modify each child's natural disposition, but to enhance and cultivate it so that it will not degenerate and he will fulfill his capabilities and develop all his potential powers. It is in this manner that nature is perfected by education.

VI *Psychology of Character Education*

The teacher must be cautioned that before undertaking the development of character it is vital to bide one's time patiently until the child's natural character becomes apparent, and then seize the opportunity of enhancing it. Otherwise one may do great damage by attempting to develop the wrong kind of personality. "To one nature it is necessary to give wings, and to another shackles; one should be spurred forward, another reined in; one should be encouraged, another intimidated; sometimes to stimulate, other times to hold in check. One man is so formed as to pursue knowledge to its ultimate course; to another it is even dangerous to learn to read. . . . There is no such thing as education before the understanding is ripe for instruction."[24] It is essential, first of all, to wait for reason to dawn, since reason is necessary for character to develop in its true form.

At birth each person comes into the world as a kind of genius endowed with talents and with a character that is peculiar to his own nature; his basic equipment consists of his innate capacities. Many people, of course, enjoy living in rustic simplicity, and they can find happiness without full development of all their faculties and potential skills. For people living in urban centers, however, it is crucial that they exploit their innate talents and every capacity endowed by nature in order to cope with conditions of city life. "In a polished society, where the head is of more use than the hands, it is necessary that all capacities nature has bestowed on men should be exploited by directing them where they can proceed furthest, and by encouraging their natural propensities in every manner that can render them useful."[25] When the good of the species is the only consideration, then educational programs call for uniformity of behavior so that everyone follows the same example or model, individuals do not employ special talents but do things by habit, and people think only ideas common to all members of the group. However, when the individual rather than the species is the primary consideration, then it is absolutely necessary for education to cultivate each talent a person has, especially the aptitudes in which he excels, and to develop his natural capacity to its highest degree. Education should be so carefully planned that it will even succeed in discovering the one person with requisite abilities for world leadership and develop him into the greatest of men.

Actually, the method of education to be utilized in the early years of childhood is identical for children possessing superior qualities and for those with less capacity. Indeed, during the very early years, the rural child ought not to be educated at all, since he is better off that way, and, as for the city child, it is best to hold his education in abeyance until one can ascertain what type of instruction is most suitable in the light of his natural bent. In all cases, however, education must not interfere with physical growth nor attempt to train the intellect before the child's reasoning power manifests itself.

To follow in the direction of natural talents of an individual is one thing, but it is quite another to discern them in every instance. In early childhood the outward indications of interest and potential achievement can be deceptive, for children often tend to imitate adults and thereby subordinate or negate their true innate propensities. The child's penchant toward a particular type of activity does not necessarily indicate a genuine interest or talent. One criterion of the latter factor is the degree of simplicity and directness; an insincere interest frequently expresses itself in the form of restlessness, overactivity, and ostentatiousness, reflecting merely a superficial aim with no real basis for achievement.

The most important aspect of child training has been neglected, that is, educating him so that he will realize his weakness and dependence, understanding "the heavy yoke of necessity that nature has imposed on mankind; and that, not only in order to make him appreciate how much is done to alleviate the burden of that yoke, but especially to instruct him betimes in what rank providence has placed him, so that he may not presume to rise by himself, or be ignorant of the reciprocal duties of humanity."[26] A young person who always has his way and all sorts of attention paid to him expects every concession in order to satisfy his fancies. Such a person enters the world of practical affairs with insolent prejudice, but is rudely awakened by humiliating experiences, confrontation, and chagrin. The right way to train a child so that he will suffer as little as possible from life's disappointments is to let him, during the early years, experience denial of his whims. Accustom him to refusals, but keep the disappointment minimal and get him used to it gradually. "To spare him long-continued fretting and rebellion, I made every refusal irrevocable. I refused him as rarely as possible, it is true, and never without due consideration."[27] There must be no capitulation to the child's importunate demands, his tears and coaxings notwithstanding, but whenever a request is granted, this must be done graciously and unconditionally.

At the first word he accepts his lot and grieves no more on seeing a box of sweets closed that he wanted to eat than on seeing a bird he would like to catch fly away: experiencing the same impossibility of having the one as having the other. A thing that has been taken away from him only appears to him something he is not able to keep, and a thing refused to him only means something he is not able to get. He would no more think of striking a person who resisted him than of striking the table on which he has hurt himself. In everything that displeases him, he feels the law of necessity, the effect of his own weakness.[28]

Either paying serious attention or yielding to screaming children reinforces their behavior, whereas letting them weep an entire day may well provide satisfactory conditioning or negative conditioning. Ill-timed indulgence results in development of a headstrong, obstinate child. "The very cause that makes him a bawler at three years of age, will make him stubborn and refractory at twelve, quarrelsome at twenty, imperious and insolent at thirty, and unbearable all his life."[29]

The exercise of authority is more effective than persuasion because the child receiving his rewards or refusals from an authoritative source knows that they have a rational basis and that he need not inqure about particular reasons for them. Once a parent yields to the judgment of a child, the child presumes to pass judgment on everything. He becomes sophistic and insincere, all too readily quibbling in order to silence others who succumb to his petty wit, and eventually he will maneuver the teacher into offering rational explanations for anything which exceeds his comprehension. If there is proper use of authority, however, all that the child need know is that he is loved and that his parent or teacher does not want him hurt. For the same reason children should not be permitted to participate in the conversation of adults.

Can it be, says she [Julie], with impatience, that we restrict their liberty by preventing them from trespassing on ours? Cannot they be truly happy unless a whole company was sitting silently admiring their puerilities? To prevent the development of their vanity is the surest means to effect their happiness; for the vanity of man is the source of his greatest miseries, and there is no person worthy of greatness and admiration whose vanity has not brought him more pain than pleasure.[30]

The false applause accorded a child is misdirected.

Questions children raise, however, are not to be avoided or forbidden when politely asked, although it is true that they need not know all things and should not be granted the privilege of inquiring concerning everything. "Generally speaking, they learn more by the questions which are asked of them than from those which they ask of others."[31]

The common practice of permitting children to pose questions to adults is not so valuable as people suppose, and should never be tolerated at the expense of their learning modesty and discretion. "What is the good of children having unlimited freedom of speech before the age of speech? Of the right of impertinently obliging persons to answer their blatant questions?"[32] Such liberty makes a child vain and foolish, and even if it is sometimes more effective than courteous listening in training him to become articulate on reaching the age of reason, nevertheless self-control and silence will at least not contribute to the narrowmindedness fostered by the habit of always blurting out things better left unsaid. Silence is golden, never despicable like the verbosity of a fool who later must regret his utterances.

VII *Natural Stages of Growth*

What must be kept in mind is that a child is a child, not a mature man, hence must be so treated. "I do not presume to aim at making them men."[33] Considerable difference exists between the person of six and the twenty-year-old. It is not one's duty to educate children, "but to prepare them for being educated."[34] The well-trained children are cheerful, happy, and less troublesome. "The only laws imposed on them in our company are those of liberty itself,"[35] viz., not to place any greater constraint on the company than the company exerts on him, not to talk louder than the person speaking, and not to demand unwarranted special attention. The sole punishment for misbehavior is dismissal from the group, and there is no other restraint placed upon the child. "They are never compelled to learn anything; never tire them with fruitless corrections; never reprimand them."[36] It is necessary to await the dawn of reason before engaging in studies that require intellectual ability. "Nothing is less necessary than for a man to be a scholar, and nothing more necessary than for him to be wise and just. . . . I am desirous to accustom them from an early age to fill their heads with ideas, and not with words; for that reason I never make them learn anything by heart."[37] Not even the children's prayers are to be learned by rote memory, but only by hearing the mother pray. The children must never be taught by means of the catechism since it is important to teach them in accordance with their natural interests and disposition.

Children's liberty is not to be restricted, nor should they abuse their liberty. "Their character can be neither corrupted nor perverted; their bodies are left to grow, and their judgments to ripen at ease and leisure."[38] Their ethical safeguard is the moral atmosphere in which they live, examples to follow, models after which to pattern themselves. Vices they have never seen will not be acquired, prejudices unknown to them will remain unknown, and passions never subject to arousal will remain unfelt. Nurtured in natural simplicity, they are free of evil tendencies. "Their ignorance is not opinionated; their desires are not obdurate; their propensity to evil is prevented, nature is justified, and everything serves to convince me that the defects we accuse her of are not those of nature but our own."[39] Vicious words are foreign weeds that must be uprooted. The work of nature unaided can educate the well-born child.

VIII *Relation of Education to other Aspects of Life*

Rousseau urges that the family be accepted as the paradigm for the proper social and political structure, since the family is truly a natural social and political organization. Each person must learn what his talent is and work at whatever pursuit is best for him so that he will be happy in his vocation. In the family, children are obligated to obey parental authority, just as the citizen is expected to obey civil authorities. But obedience will be obtained by awakening the child's sense of duty rather than by the use of force. The principle of the social contract governs relationships within each family as well as those in the nation viewed as a larger family. Julie's ideas on education are based on the same social contract principle.

Human civilization has its youth and maturity as does an individual person. The direction of civilization will depend upon the implementation of basic educational principles as applied to the individual. In each human being, impulses and sentiments precede reason, as the body precedes the mind. Consequently the training of the body should be given priority over that of the mind. Each person has his particular natural bent as well as a constitution shared with others. The individual's native equipment should be developed through education and perfected; and in so doing one need not fear the consequences, for nature makes no mistakes. The proper type of education merely continues and brings to fruition what nature has begun. Thus the development of character cannot proceed until the individual's personality matures and observable character traits begin to appear. Character formation, fundamental to progress not only in education and the home but throughout the society depends upon natural forces. Rousseau repeats his plea for a return to nature which imposes the necessity for self-restraint and discipline and his reminder that religious education cannot be carried on by means of a catechism or rote learning. True Christians are not developed by such means.

CHAPTER 5

Emile (Books I-IV)—Education as the Art of Forming Men

Emile is Rousseau's classic on the philosophy of education, his definitive work, containing ideas already expressed in the *New Heloise,* but in much more systematic form. There are other differences. Whereas in the *New Heloise,* Julie educates her own children, in the *Emile* the boy receives private instruction from an imaginary tutor. A further difference is that Julie's children are young throughout, whereas Emile's education is traced from early childhood to manhood, from the age of six years to maturity.

Emile's is a carefully planned program of education in a dyadic society consisting most often of himself and his tutor whose responsibility it is to pursue "the progress of infancy and the course natural to the human heart." Precautions are taken to prevent outside influences from perverting the original goodness of the boy. The prescribed form of education designed for Emile is suitable only for well-to-do people, for Rousseau believed that the poor need only a limited education useful in their economic situation. But one aim of Emile's education is to make certain that he remains free of the deeply rooted class prejudice extremely prevalent among eighteenth-century noblemen. Emile's experiences are in many respects similar to those of Rousseau during his own boyhood. There was no mother in the home. Emile's situation was not unlike that of an orphan given over to a tutor's care, inasmuch as his father was also the tutor whom the boy must respect and obey at all times.

Rousseau was well aware that Emile's situation was an ideal one virtually impossible to duplicate in life, but he felt that the methods of instruction delineated for Emile would effectively elucidate his philosophy of education and that, moreover, many of them would be feasible and successful in numerous situations.

I *The Plan for Emile's Education*

Rousseau had only a short-lived unsatisfactory teaching experience, but he habitually observed the behavior of children with critical eyes and recalled vividly his own miseducation during childhood. Consequently it is not surprising that he developed pedagogical theories about the proper education of Emile that were antithetical to the methods which had been applied to himself.

In accordance with his faith in all works of nature, Rousseau portrayed Emile as a child born innocent, hence natively good. In direct opposition to the natively good individual is society with its artificial, antagonistic institutions and customs, from which the child must be protected. How is this result to be effected? By negative education, a technique that must be utilized at least until the child attains the age of twelve years. There must be no didactic teaching nor authoritative adult prescriptions of moral standards, no resort to punishments or rewards. Parental authority must be suppressed if the laws of nature and the natural influences upon the child are to take effect. Nevertheless, despite this injunction, education in the home is preferable to training away from the influence of family life; Rousseau cited the advantages associated with family relationships and the lessons to be learned from the fulfillment of reciprocal obligations within the family.

He arrived at a rather arbitrary division into four periods demarcating childhood and adolescence and noted the appropriate characteristics of each developmental period. One must not attempt, he said, to "manufacture" men out of children; they must be treated as children whose development progresses only in so far as they are self-taught. Moral and religious training must await the period of adolescence.

II *Stages of Educational Development*

One of the most significant contributions of Rousseau to the philosophy of education is his concept of natural developmental stages peculiar to the different periods of life from infancy to adulthood. Each period requires its own pedagogical approach so that, for example, an infant will not be treated as a child, nor a child as an adolescent. The various developmental periods as Rousseau saw them are as follows: (1) infancy; (2) childhood; (3) boyhood or preadolescence; (4) adolescence or youth; and (5) manhood. The first period extends from birth to two years of age, the second from two to twelve, the third from twelve to fifteen, the fourth from fifteen to twenty (or to the age of marriage beyond twenty); and the fifth from twenty (or the marriage age) through adulthood.

In infancy the child is virtually an animal like other animals; in the second period he is a savage; in the third period he acquires self-sufficiency and intelligence; and in the fourth he exhibits a soul, that is, a conscience, social outlook, sex interests, and the personalization of values of truth, beauty, and goodness. (The fifth period, manhood, is the consummation of education in the preceding four periods.) Virtue is now within reach, and his life is ruled by conscience. Thus education must be conducted so that the proper experiences will be provided for each group on the basis of age.

The first stage is keynoted by physical and social training, during which a golden mean between neglect and overindulgence of the child prevails. Negative education dominates the second stage. Nature study and science constitute the main program in the third. Academic studies become important in the fourth period together with training in control over the emotions, the study of history and religion (at eighteen years of age), and social relationships learned from social contacts, great literature, and the theater. Thereafter Emile finds the ideal woman whom he eventually marries, but not before travelling to see the world and studying its political institutions. Education is now at an end.

III *Education during Stage One: Infancy*

When in the Preface to the *Emile* Rousseau wrote: "as for public usefulness, the most useful of all arts, the art of forming men, is still neglected," he was offering his definition of education. He protested against the common practice of teachers in teaching a child what a man is expected to know, without regard for the child's learning capabilities. "They are always looking for the man in the child," and fail to consider that a child is a child with his own immature nature quite different from that of an adult.

Rousseau opened his *Emile, on Education as the Art of Forming Men* (often translated as *Emile, or a Treatise on Education*), with the attention-commanding sentence: "God makes all things good; man meddles with them and they become evil." In effect, man forces "one tree to bear another's fruit." He mutilates what is natural as if he loved what is deformed. Society makes use of prejudice, authority, compulsion, and example to stifle a person's nature. "Plants are fashioned by cultivation, man by education."[1] Education is derived from nature, men, and things, three educative sources which must co-operate for the best results, but the only one subject to human control is men. Since nature is uncontrollable, education must conform to it.

Nature is essentially habit; "education itself is but habit."[2] Education is therefore properly defined as "habits conformable to nature."[3] Inasmuch as natural man lives for himself rather than for others (society), the choice must be made "between man and the citizen, for you cannot train both."

The philosophy of education considers man and his total environment. "Those of us who can best endure the good and evil of life are the best educated; hence it follows that true education consists less in precept than in practice. We begin to learn when we begin to live."[4] Education begins with one's self at birth, and one's nurse is his first teacher.

Nature is the infant's real teacher, however, instructing the child in the meaning of grief and pain by exposing him to many hardships endured in growing up. "The child who has overcome hardships has gained strength.... This is nature's law."[5] The ability of a child to endure change surpasses that of the adult, with pain as the means of his preservation. The seeds of passion are sown early in the lifetime of an infant, and he is thereafter trained to be aggressive like a tyrant or submissive like a slave, destined to rule if parents accede to his wishes or to obey if they insist on obedience.

The father should be his child's tutor, instead of hiring a mercenary to take his place, and the mother should be the child's nurse. A classroom crowded with students is no place for the education of any pupil, for "one man can only educate one pupil."[6] As for knowledge to be taught an infant, there is only one thing to know—duty! Parents should bear in mind that for the child to develop into a citizen of the world he will have to live in a temperate climate and commune with nature.

According to Rousseau, education is only for the children of the wealthy, and the type of education he designed is a type which only a rich man can afford.

The poor man has no need of education. The education of his own station in life is forced upon him, and he can have no other; but the education received by the rich man from his own station is least fitted for himself and for society. Moreover, a natural education should fit a man for any position.[7]

Consequently the person Rousseau selected to exemplify his ideal educational program was the rich orphan Emile, rich because the poor neither need nor can afford a private tutor, male because a woman requires an entirely different education as an ancillary to the male, orphaned because interference by parents is undesirable. Rousseau commented: "Let us choose our scholar among the rich; we shall at least have made another man; the poor may come to manhood without our help."[8]

Like the marriage contract, nature is a party to the marriage; therefore all burdens imposed by nature, such as illness, must be borne with fortitude. Just as it is desirable to have a strong servant, so "the body must be strong enough to obey the mind. . . . A feeble body makes a feeble mind."[9] Rousseau's pupil has no need of the rules of physicians, the precepts of philosophers, or the exhortations of theologians, all of whom debase the heart by putting it in terror of death. In order to develop the child into a brave man, place him in a setting where neither physicians nor the ravages of disease can be seen. "In the course of nature, a man bears pain bravely and dies in peace."[10] Medicine is a lying art, useless to body and mind, an invention designed to infest the mind with illness. Rather than curing people, physicians infect the mind with the lethal disorders of cowardice, timidity, heightened suggestibililty, and fear of death. "I do not deny that medicine is useful to some men; I assert that it is fatal to mankind."[11] Rousseau refused to accept anyone as a pupil unless he were strong and healthy.

A weak body is vulnerable to many evils and ills; consequently a strong body is desirable and necessary for effective development. "The weaker the body, the more imperious its demands; the stronger it is, the better it obeys."[12] In the course of time, temperance, by stimulating the passions, has deleterious effects, while fasting and penance produce similar results by awakening excessive appetites. "All sensual passions find their home in effeminate bodies; the less satisfaction they can get the keener is their sting."[13] It is evident from those who have lived longest that exercise is essential to longevity and the prevention of disease.

Rousseau, noting that people are destroyed by urban living conditions, advocated the fresh air of the country for building up the constitution of the child. From the time that the child draws his first breath, he must be liberated from caps, bandages, swaddling clothes, and every other means of restraint. Infants are not to be confused with mature persons, hence must be approached differently. Even if a child were actually born with the brain of an adult, this "child-man would be a perfect idiot, an automaton, a statue without motion and almost without feeling; he would see and hear nothing, he would recognize no one."[14] It is only the capability of learning with which a person is born, not knowledge or preception. In this respect Rousseau was influenced by Locke's concept of the *tabula rasa* (blank tablet) mind. The infant's movements and cries, he urged, are purely reflex, devoid of knowledge or will. "Man's education begins at birth; before he can speak or understand he is learning. Experience precedes instructions; when he recognizes his nurse he has learnt much."[15] The infant with his numerous needs should be protected against the addition of habit as a fresh need. "The only habit the child should be allowed to contract is that of having no habits."[16] It is advisable, therefore, from the beginning to carry the child on either arm in order to prevent his becoming accustomed to a favored position, and to see that he is not unable to be left alone either day or night. "Prepare the way for his control of liberty and the use of his strength by allowing his body its natural habit, by making him capable of lasting self-control, of doing all that he wills when his will is formed."[17]

Since natural man is interested in whatever is new and unfamiliar, allow the infant to see things that are new and unfamiliar (provided there are no ill effects) so that his fear of the unknown will vanish. Note that it is not the peasant child, but the one reared in a clean home, who develops a fear of spiders. Two centuries ago Rousseau's keen interest in the psychology of learning enabled him to anticipate many findings of behavior psychology and behavior psychotherapy that are in vogue today. He was fully aware of the need for training the child to refine his sensitivity to situations and experiences. The following advice is typical:

All children are afraid of masks. I begin by showing Emile a mask with a pleasant face, then some one puts this mask before his face: I begin to laugh, they all laugh too, and the child with them. By degrees I accustom him to less pleasing masks, and at last hideous ones. If I have arranged my stages skilfully, far from being afraid of the last mask, he will laugh at it as he did at the first. After that I am not afraid that people will frighten him with masks.[18]

Rousseau's educational theory has amazingly modern overtones.

A strong child is not only healthy but well prepared to

learn, and he has a marked preference for high standards of morality. "All wickedness comes from weakness. The child is naughty only because he is weak; make him strong and he will be good; if we could do everything, we would never do wrong,"[19] as is true in the case of almighty God. Note also that the stronger nations regard evil as inferior to good. Accordingly Rousseau formulated four pedagogical principles or maxims:

First Maxim.—Far from being too strong, children are not strong enough for all the claims of nature. Give them full use of such strength as they have; they will not abuse it.
Second Maxim.—Help them and supply the experience and strength they lack whenever the need is of the body.
Third Maxim.—In the help you give them confine yourself to what is really needful, without granting anything to caprice or unreason; for they will not be tormented by caprice if you do not call it into existence, seeing it is no part of nature.
Fourth Maxim.—Study carefully their speech and gestures, so that at an age when they are incapable of deceit you may discriminate between those desires which come from nature and those which spring from perversity.[20]

These rules are calculated to allow granting greater genuine liberty with less power to children so that they will be able to fend for themselves without making demands on others.

It is inadvisable to offer caresses as a substitute for a cure in illnesses such as colic, for the infant will thus be taught the erroneous idea that he must suffer in order to gain rewards such as affection, and he will use that idea to gain control over you with the result that his entire education will be ruined. When his own obstinacy instead of genuine need drives an infant to tears, distracting his attention with something pleasant is a wise remedy.

Since the child should think ideas rather than words, a limited vocabulary is no cause for alarm.

The infant is progressing in several ways at once; he is learning to talk, eat, and walk about the same time. This is really the first phase of his life. Up till now, he was little more than he was before birth; he had neither feeling nor thought, he was barely capable of sensation; he was unconscious of his own existence.[21]

Infancy ends and childhood begins when the child learns to speak instead of crying, for "one language supplants another." This progression from infancy to childhood as the second stage of life is a natural transition.

IV *Education during Stage Two: Childhood*

Noting that infancy is the period devoid of oral communication, Rousseau maintained that childhood commences with the ability to speak. Parents must be on guard against providing excessive care, but kindness is the first duty of everyone, for acts of kindness reflect the greatest wisdom. "Love childhood, indulge in its sports, its pleasures, its delightful instincts."[22]

Do not inflict upon the child more disappointments than his condition warrants. People will never know any absolute good and evil, since in this life the two are adulterated. Happiness and suffering are experiences common to everyone, the happiest person being he who suffers least and the most miserable being he who enjoys least. "Man's happiness in this world is but a negative state; it must be reckoned by the fewness of his ills."[23] What makes a man wretched is the disproportionality existing between his desires and his powers. "A conscious being whose powers were equal to his desires would be perfectly happy."[24] Hypothetically it would follow that a person whose power was absolute would be absolutely happy. "True happiness consists in decreasing the difference between our desires and our powers, in establishing a perfect equilibrium between the power and the will."[25] Otherwise a person can never expect to be happy.

Nature, doing everything for the best, grants a person only those desires that are necessary for his self-preservation, and man's powers are such as to satisfy these desires. "The nearer we are to pleasure the further we are from happiness. On the other hand, the more nearly a man's condition approximates this state of nature the less difference is there between his desires and his powers, and happiness is therefore less remote. Lacking everything, he is never less miserable; for misery consists, not in the lack of things, but in the needs which they inspire."[26] While the world of imagination is limitless, reality has its bounds, the miseries people suffer arising from a discrepancy between their real and imaginary worlds. Actually life's goods are merely matters of opinion, excepting health, strength, and conscience. Excluding physical suffering and remorse, a person's woes are imaginary.

An endless life on earth is not to be desired, nor would anyone accept the "sorrowful gift" of immortality if it were granted to him.

Human institutions are one mass of folly and contradiction. As our life loses its value we set a higher price upon it. The old regret life more than the young; they do not want to lose all they have spent in preparing for its enjoyment. At sixty it is cruel to die when one has not begun to live. Man is credited with a strong desire for self-preservation, and this desire exists; but we fail to perceive that this desire, as felt by us, is largely the work of man. In a natural state man is only eager to preserve his life while he has the means for its preservation; when self-preservation is no longer possible, he resigns himself to his fate and dies without vain torments. Nature teaches us the first law of resignation. Savages, like wild beasts, make very little struggle against death, and meet it almost without a murmur. When this natural law is overthrown reason establishes another, but few discern it, and man's resignation is never so complete as nature's.[27]

Prudence, the source of all man's troubles, is the culprit bidding a person to peer into his future, an unattainable one. The error of looking forward to the future is that the present is neglected. One denies himself today for an uncertain future.

To avoid being wretched it is necessary to live one's own life, and every person has his appointed place in nature, in the order of things. Accordingly the individual should accept the law of necessity by permitting his freedom and power to exceed his natural strength. To do so is to become a victim of slavery, trickery, and deceit. No one really gets his own way unless he learns how to obtain it singlehanded. Not power but freedom is man's greatest good, the truly free man being he who desires only what he can achieve and does that which he desires. Rousseau, affirming this as his fundamental maxim because all the rules of education arise therefrom, considered it imperative to apply his maxim to childhood education. "Society has enfeebled man, not merely by robbing him of the right to his own strength, but still more by making his strength insufficient for his needs. This is why his desires increase in proportion to his weakness."[28] This observation also explains why the child is weaker than the adult. The reason is not that a man's strength is greater by nature, but that the adult can provide for himself, whereas the child's desires are caprices (spurious desires not based on genuine needs) requiring the assistance of others for their fulfillment.

Rousseau's educational reforms are based upon utilitarian grounds. "No one, not even his father, has the right to bid the child do what is of no use to him."[29] The best course to take in education is to guide the child so that he will be dependent, not on persons, but on things, for it is natural to be dependent on the physical world, unnatural to be enslaved to persons. Provided that human prejudices or social institutions have not interfered with a person's natural tendencies, happiness will be found to be (both in children and adults) the enjoyment of one's liberty. "He who does as he likes is happy provided he is self-sufficient; it is so with the man who is living in a state of nature."[30] If a child's desires exceed his strength then he will be unhappy despite doing what he likes. The inability to dispense with the assistance of others renders a person weak and wretched.

"Nature provides for the child's growth in her own fashion, and this should never be thwarted."[31] Consequently a child should not be forced to remain seated when he craves physical activity. Frustrating a child causes the state of caprice. Avoid teaching the child insincere phrases of politeness that merely serve as a weapon for him to maneuver another into obtaining his own selfish way. Such artificial education renders the child politely impervious, providing him with an instrument that others cannot resist.

Rousseau contended that the slight hardships endured by his pupil were more than compensated by the liberty he enjoyed. It is unnatural to protect a person from certain kinds of suffering. "Do you think any man can find true happiness elsewhere than in his natural state: and when you try to spare him all suffering, are you not taking him out of his natural state?"[32] Excessive prosperity is morally corrupting, and granting a child his every wish contributes to his misery because "his wants increase in proportion to the ease with which they are satisfied."

The first erroneous notions that the child acquires are those pertaining to error and vice; hence he must be carefully watched in this respect. "Before the age of reason it is impossible to form any idea of moral beings or social relations."[33] Wrong ideas obtained at a young age are virtually impossible to erase. Thus moral training should await the age of reason.

Nature would have them children before they are men. If we try to invert this order we shall produce a forced fruit immature and flavourless, fruit which will be rotten before it is ripe; we shall have young doctors and old children. Childhood has its own ways of seeing, thinking, and feeling; nothing is more foolish than to try and substitute our ways; and I should no more expect judgment in a ten-year-old child than I should expect him to be five feet high.[34]

The understanding of duty is beyond the child at this age; all that he need know is that natural impulses are invariably correct inasmuch as original sin does not exist. Self-love is the only natural passion and is in itself good. "Until the time is ripe for the appearance of reason, that guide of selfishness, the main thing is that the child shall do nothing because you are watching him or listening to him; in a word, nothing because of other people, but only what nature asks of him; then he will never do wrong."[35] The reason that a child can do considerable damage without committing wrong is the fact that in him harmful intentions are absent and not as yet cultivated; accordingly articles that the young child can destroy should be removed from his reach. Even though he learns from experience, he does not need to experience a clear and present evil of decadent society but can learn to avoid it by proper action of parents and teachers. On the other hand, if he breaks a window pane, he must still sleep in his cold room and learn the consequences of what has happened.

Emile will be brought up in the country. living in a typical room of peasants that will require no embellishments since he will rarely spend any time in it, his most important rule of education being: "Do not save time, but lose it."[36] (Many such striking paradoxes are to be found in Rousseau's works.) Life's most precarious period occurs between birth and the age of twelve years.

Education of the earliest years should be merely negative. It consists, not in teaching virtue or truth, but in preserving the heart from vice and from the spirit of error. If only you could let well alone, and get others to follow your example; if you could bring your scholar to the age of twelve strong and healthy, but unable to tell his right hand from his left, the eyes of his understanding would be open to reason as soon as you began to teach him. Free from prejudices and free from habits, there would be nothing in him to counteract the effect of your labours. In your hands he would be the wisest of men; by doing nothing to begin with, you would end with a prodigy of education.

Reverse the usual practice and you will almost always do right.[37]

Before training a man, said Rousseau, it is necessary that you yourself be a man, an acceptable model. Another important consideration is the "child's individual bent, which must be thoroughly known before one can choose the most suitable moral training. Every mind has its own form."[38] One's first duty is to himself, inasmuch as justice arises from what is owed to the self rather than what is due to others. "It is impossible to train a child up to the age of twelve in the midst of society."[39] Resorting to punishment should be strictly prohibited since nature herself attends to it so that punishment is the natural consequence of the act committed.

Children's lies are the work of their teachers, for a child cannot tell a lie in making a promise since he is unaware of its significance. Virtues acquired by imitation are appropriate only for monkeys; imitation is rooted in one's desire to escape from himself. "The noblest virtues are negative,"[40] and therefore the most important moral lesson is: "Never hurt anybody." One should not be hasty in his judgment of children, but should "hold childhood in reverence."

Because children are devoid of true memory, they are incapable of making judgments. Of course, they do have a sort of rational thinking, but it is limited by their lack of a language prior to attaining the age of reason. "Minds are formed by language, thoughts take their colour from its ideas."[41] However, language should not be taught in the earliest years. "You will be surprised to find that I reckon the study of languages among the useless lumber of education."[42] Teachers master dead languages to disguise their own deficiencies in the native tongue. Geography and, even more so, history are ridiculous subjects to teach, for a child does not understand symbols and cannot read a map, and history is a set of facts in the child's mind devoid of the necessary cause-and-effect relationships that make them meaningful. "Emile will not learn anything by heart, not even fables. . . . Men may be taught by fables; children require the naked truth."[43]

Without a knowledge of words, basic to ideas, all studies are unsuitable, and a mind devoid of ideas has no real memory.

When I thus get rid of children's lessons, I get rid of the chief cause of their sorrows, namely their books. Reading is the curse of childhood, yet it is almost the only occupation you can find for children. Emile, at twelve years of age, will hardly know what a book is.[44]

Only when reading affords utilitarian value should the teacher resort to such instruction; otherwise it is a nuisance. "As for my pupil, or rather nature's pupil, he has been trained from the outset to be as self-reliant as possible. . . . Nature, not man, is his schoolmaster, and he learns all the quicker because he is not aware that he has any lesson to learn."[45] The educational structure should be one in which the child rather than the teacher is master; and though the teacher really exercises ultimate control, the pupil should feel that he himself is in charge.

Cognizant of the limitations of his educational theory, Rousseau expressed the following reservations:

The more I urge my method of letting well alone, the more objections I perceive against it. If your pupil learns nothing from you, he will learn from others. If you do not instill truth he will learn falsehoods; the prejudices you fear to teach him he will acquire from those about him, they will find their way through every one of his senses; they will either corrupt his reason before it is fully developed or his mind will become torpid through inaction, and will become engrossed in material things. If we do not form the habit of thinking as children, we shall lose the power of thinking for the rest of our life.[46]

Like the cat sniffing about examining everything in sight, so the child must be educated by properly using his inquisitive instinct. The teacher must motivate the pupil to do everything the teacher wants "without bidding him or forbidding him to do anything."

Clothing, too, is an important pedagogical consideration, the desirable dress being that which affords the most comfort and freedom. "Before the child is enslaved by our prejudices his first wish is always to be free and comfortable."[47] Children are usually overwrapped in clothing, but Emile wears little or no covering on his head even in the winter. Children require considerable rest after violent exercise, but they must learn to sleep in uncomfortable beds. "A hard life, when once we have become used to it, increases our pleasant experiences; an easy life prepares the way for innumerable unpleasant experiences."[48] For the child who instantly falls asleep, no pillow is too hard, and the best bed for him is the one in which he obtains the best sleep. Sometimes Emile was awakened abruptly in order to accustom him to all sorts of conditions. Even games and sports have lessons to teach. "The sports of the young savage involve long fasting, blows, burns, and fatigue of every kind, a proof that even pain has a charm of its own, which may remove its bitterness."[49] Man should not become enslaved to pain. In order to overcome fear of the dark, many games should be played in the dark, for habit overpowers the intimidation of imagination. Just as the experienced tiler working on a roof no longer becomes dizzy, so the child accustomed to the dark has become unafraid. One good way to help a child to overcome his fear of the dark is to put him in a dark room and let him listen to people laughing and talking in an adjoining room.

Pupils should enjoy their work. For Emile, "work or play

are all one to him, his games are his work; he knows no difference."[50] Food should be simple and plain, with children eating as much as their appetite requires. "Our appetite is excessive only because we try to impose on it rules other than those of nature."[51] With this observation Rousseau ended his discussion of education in Stage Two, the main period of childhood.

V *Education during Stage Three: Preadolescence*

During childhood years there is a period of weakness caused by a disproportionate relationship between the child's strength and his needs. In other words, his passions are responsible for weakness because he has insufficient natural strength to obtain satisfaction of his needs. Either his strength must be augmented or his desires curbed if he is to resolve the matter. At about twelve years of age, however, a period of life begins in which strength increases, even to the point of exceeding the amount necessary; it is a period of approaching adolescence, i.e., it is the period of preadolescence. During preadolescence, from twelve to fifteen years of age, a stage which Rousseau still referred to as childhood because his pupil was only approaching adolescence, not having reached the age of puberty, "the child's strength increases far more rapidly than his needs."[52] During this period

the strongest and fiercest of the passions is still unknown, his physical development is still imperfect and seems to await the call of the will. He is scarcely aware of extremes of heat and cold and braves them with impunity. He needs no coat, his blood is warm; no spices, hunger is his sauce, no food comes amiss at this age; if he is sleepy he stretches himself on the ground and goes to sleep; he finds all he needs within his reach; he is not tormented by any imaginary wants; he cares nothing what others think; his desires are not beyond his grasp; not only is he self-sufficing, but for the first and last time in his life he has more strength than he needs.[53]

If this statement is somewhat exaggerated, at least it must be admitted that the preadolescent experiences both less of passions than the adult and less of wants than the younger child.

Although preadolescence is a time of greatest relative strength, for the child's strength exceeds his wants, it is of all-too-brief duration and occurs but once. However, "it is the most precious time in his life," with "a surplus of strength and capacity which he will never have again."[54] It is a time for instruction and inquiry requiring both hands and head, a time to select what must be taught. Beware, said Rousseau, lest the intoxication of pride lead to error. "Keep this truth ever before you—Ignorance never did any one any harm, error alone is fatal, and we do not lose our way through ignorance but through self-confidence."[55] It is a time to avoid the teaching of truths meant for the understanding of a fully matured mind such as instruction in interpersonal relations or social relations, for the immature mind will acquire a mistaken interpretation of them.

Up to the time of preadolescence the child is governed by the principle of necessity; during preadolescence he is guided by the principle of utility; and moral or philosophical principles do not play a major role until later in life. "See how we are gradually approaching the moral ideas which distinguish between good and evil. Hitherto we have known no law but necessity, now we are considering what is useful; we shall soon come to what is fitting and right."[56] Man's instinct, which innervates his diverse powers, initially seeks an outlet through physical activity and only later expends its energy in mental activity requiring knowledge.

Even if a person with a scientific bent were left on an island with his books and instruments, he would explore his environment before resorting to them. In like manner the preadolescent must follow his instincts to the things he is impelled to study, viz., those objects that excite his senses rather than his abstract reasoning. Let him explore his island, for the intellectual world is still beyond him; it is the visible horizons with which he must deal.

Let us transform our sensations into ideas, but let us not jump all at once from the objects of sense to objects of thought. The latter are attained by means of the former. Let the senses be the only guide for the first workings of reason. No book but the world, no teaching but that of fact. The child who reads ceases to think, he only reads. He is acquiring words not knowledge.[57]

Thus it is the phenomenon of nature that the pupil must observe so that his curiosity will be aroused and will be stimulated into activity and growth. Supply him with problems and permit him to arrive at a solution. "Let him know nothing because you have told him, but because he has learnt it for himself. Let him not be taught science, let him discover it."[58] Never substitute the statements of authority for his own reasoning, for that will signal the death of reason, rendering him "a mere plaything of other people's thoughts." Accordingly if geography is to be taught, do not have recourse to globes, symbols, maps, and spheres, but exhibit the real thing to him by taking him where he can see the wide horizon in full view for himself and note the objects marking its setting place. Begin the child's geography lesson with the town in which he lives, and let him make maps—not learn from them first, for he cannot understand symbolic instruction. "Never substitute the symbol for the thing signified, unless it is impossible to show the thing itself," and "never tell the child what he cannot understand: no descriptions, no eloquence, no figures of speech, no poetry."[59] For the child nothing is good excepting what he himself recognizes as good; therefore do not tell him what to do, for that he must find out for himself and act autonomously. (Rousseau recommended but one book, *Robinson Crusoe*, because it describes "life according to nature.")

Although Rousseau accepted the Aristotelian philosophy of eudaimonism, which makes happiness man's supreme goal, he differed with Aristotle as to the nature of happiness. He viewed happiness as negative, as the absence of pain; its characteristics are the possessions of health, freedom, and life's necessities. Moral happiness is also an important consideration. Although everyone desires happiness, few know what it is, for it is found in the naturalness of the simple life.

Emile must learn a trade, for manual labor is the type most similar to labor in a state of nature, and the artisan is dependent on good luck for his success. Only the man who knows a trade is a free man because he depends entirely upon himself and his own labor. Ill-treat the man with a trade and he is free to move where he will.

Learning a trade matters less than overcoming the prejudices of people who despise the trade. You will never be reduced to earning your livelihood; so much the worse for you. No matter; work for honour, not for need; stoop to the position of a working man, to rise above your own. To conquer fortune and everything else, begin by independence. To rule through public opinion, begin by ruling over it.

Remember I demand no talent, only a trade, a genuine trade, a mere mechanical art, in which the hands work harder than the head, a trade which does not lead to fortune but makes you independent of her.[60]

Even a lord, a marquis, or a prince may lose his fortune some day, and for that reason Rousseau wanted to raise Emile to "a rank which he cannot lose, a rank which will always do him honour; I want to raise him to the status of a man, and, whatever you may say, he will have fewer equals in that rank than in your own."[61] Emile will maintain his dignity by having a trade, yet it should not be an unnecessary one such as that of a "wigmaker," but a useful one that is always in demand. Every pupil should master a trade befitting his sex and age. "Sedentary indoor employments, which make the body tender and effeminate, are neither pleasing nor suitable. . . . An unhealthy trade I forbid to my pupil, but not a difficult or dangerous one,"[62] for that will cultivate strength and courage in him. Carpentry is an excellent trade because it is clean, useful, offers exercise, and can be undertaken at home. Rousseau suggested that the child can best master a suitable trade in the natural course of events without even becoming aware that he is learning it. He should use his skill for the common good, for even a wealthy man is obligated to work for the benefit of the community.

During this stage of Emile's education, his knowledge has been restricted to nature and to things, while history, metaphysics, and morals are unknown to him and he has no power of generalization and abstraction. Although he is ignorant of the nature of things, he knows how he is affected by them. His values are strictly utilitarian, and he is free from prejudice. His imagination is yet asleep, but he is nevertheless courageous, industrious, temperate, patient, and steadfast. Offering no resistance to fate, he accepts the law of necessity. Not knowing the meaning of death, he accepts it as a dictate of nature, without groaning or struggling. "To live in freedom, and to be independent of human affairs, is the best way to learn how to die."[63] His virtues are restricted to himself, for mastery of social virtues must await his acquisition of knowledge about those interpersonal relations involved in them. He directs his behavior toward his own benefit, not for the benefit of others, for he neither acknowledges any debt to them nor makes any claims upon them. His errors are minimal, the inescapable ones to which everyone is heir. With an accurate mind unfettered by prejudice, a free heart undisturbed by passion, and a healthy, physically supple body, Rousseau's pupil, with scarcely any pride, arrives at his fifteenth year of age.

Emile, who formerly had only sensations, now has ideas and ceases to be a child as his ideas lend character to his mind. Whereas he once could only feel, he is now capable of reasoning.

He is more than ever conscious of the necessity which makes him dependent on things. After exercising his body and his senses you have exercised his mind and his judgment. Finally we have joined together the use of his limbs and his faculties. We have made him a worker and a thinker; we have now to make him loving and tender-hearted, to perfect reason through feeling. . . . The more we know, the more mistakes we make; therefore ignorance is the only way to escape error. Form no judgments and you will never be mistaken. This is the teaching both of nature and of reason.[64]

Inasmuch as all errors arise in consequence of a faulty judgment, learning becomes a necessity, "for had we no need for judgment, we should not need to learn,"[65] and consequently would not be subject to mistakes, hence would be happier in ignorance than in knowledge. One can find more mistaken ideas in the Academy of Sciences than in a tribe of American Indians. Although Emile knows little, "what he knows is really his own; he has no half-knowledge."[66]

VI *Educating during Stage Four: from Adolescence to Maturity*

Adolescence which, according to Rousseau, begins with puberty, is a second birth; characteristics of this period include a voice growing hoarse, sparse down upon the cheeks, and other changes in appearance. Neither boy nor man, the adolescent is born again. "We are born, so to speak, twice over; born into existence, and born into life."[67] With the second birth when no human passion is unknown, a man truly enters into life.

He is beginning to learn to lower his eyes and blush, he is becoming sensitive, though he does not know what it is that he feels; he is uneasy without knowing why. All this may happen gradually and give you time enough; but if his keenness becomes impatience, his eagerness madness, if he is angry and sorry all in a moment, if he weeps without cause, if in the presence of objects which are beginning to be a source of danger his pulse quickens and his eyes sparkle, if he trembles when a woman's hand touches his, if he is troubled or timid in her presence, O Ulysses, wise Ulysses! have a care![68]

Passions serve the purpose of self-preservation, originating in self-love as the basic, primitive instinct producing all others which are merely modifications of it. Self-love, invariably good, accords with nature. "Self-preservation requires, therefore, that we shall love ourselves; we must love ourselves above everything, and it follows directly from this that we love what contributes to our preservation."[69] However, from self-love, the child's first sentiment, there derives a second sentiment, the love he feels toward those about him. Because all are predisposed to assist the child, he, too, feels kindly toward them by nature. Self-love is not to be confused with selfishness, for "self-love, which concerns itself only with ourselves, is content to satisfy our own needs; but selfishness, which is always comparing the self with others, is never satisfied and never can be; for this feeling, which prefers ourselves to others, requires that they should prefer us to themselves, which is impossible."[70] Consequently self-love is the well-spring of the tender and gentle emotions, while selfishness is the root of despicable passions.

"Man's proper study," held Rousseau, "is that of his relation to his environment."[71] As a child Emile studied the environment by using physical equipment, i.e., his senses, examining himself in relation to things. Now, however, in his adolescence, as he is acquiring a moral nature and is becoming socialized, he studies himself "in relation to his fellow-men; this is the business of his whole life."[72]

During this period his sex life is awakened so that he is attracted to the opposite sex. "As soon as a man needs a companion he is no longer an isolated creature, his heart is no longer alone."[73] Love, too, appears at this time, but it is not produced by reason, for it is blind. Love, always held in honor by mankind, arises from time and knowledge rather than reason. "Love does not spring from nature, far from it; it is the curb and law of her desires. . . . Love must be mutual. To be loved we must be worthy of love; to be preferred we must be more worthy than the rest."[74] A heart overflowing with love requires a friend, not merely a mistress. Once experiencing love's sweetness, the feeling of being loved, a person then desires to be loved by everyone.

Discussing sex education, Rousseau, leaving nothing to chance, believed that a boy should be kept in ignorance until the age of sixteen, but, if that is not possible, then instruction should begin before the age of ten. It should be done without evoking lascivious ideas, without lying, and without arousing curiosity. "A single untruth on the part of the master will destroy the results of his education."[75] In addition to being true, answers should be brief, definite, and unhesitating. Children have neither the desires of adults nor their modesty, which, while natural to mature individuals, is not natural to the child.

It is not nature, but the voice of convention, of one's society, that arouses sexuality. For passions to be controlled and the tide of rising passions to be stemmed, the period of their development should be prolonged so that nature will awaken them at the appropriate time. Because other people, conventionality, and his surroudings inflame his imagination,

Emile's mental images must be curbed by reason and feeling. "It is the errors of the imagination which transmute into vices the passions of finite beings."[76] In order that the individual may apply his reason to stem the tide of sensuality, he will be guided by a wise teacher: "First, to be conscious of the true relations of man both in the species and the individual; second, to control all the affections in accordance with these relations."[77] Wisdom dictates that innocence be prolonged, for "young men, corrupted in early youth and .addicted to women and debauchery, are inhuman and cruel."[78] Such persons, merciless and pitiless, would sacrifice anything for the sake of their own pleasures.

In addition to kindling sex, the imagination also ignites the spark of compassion. The adolescent at the age of sixteen, having had an acquaintance with suffering, can picture the suffering of others through his powers of imagination. Touched by the cries of others, he has learned to suffer in sympathy with their sufferings; and thus pity, "the first relative sentiment which touches the human heart according to the order of nature,"[79] is born. "It is at this time that the sorrowful picture of suffering humanity should stir his heart with the first touch of pity he has ever known."[80] Three maxims summarizing Rousseau's theory of pity are:

First Maxim.—It is not in human nature to put ourselves in the place of those who are happier than ourselves, but only in the place of those who can claim our pity.
Second Maxim.—We never pity another's woes unless we know we may suffer in like manner ourselves.
Third Maxim.—The pity we feel for others is proportionate, not to the amount of the evil, but to the feelings we attribute to the sufferers."[81]

Unless one feels that another is in need of his pity, he tends to feel no pity for him.

Contrast the characters of two young men entering the world by diametrically opposite doors at the end of their early education, one of whom is a child of civilization, while the other is Rousseau's adolescent pupil, a child of nature. The former is never truly happy, is indeed perpetually discontented. If someone is better dressed than himself, he is disturbed; if he himself is the better dressed, he discovers the other person's superiority over him with respect to birth, intellect, or some other disturbing feature. Insults and humiliations must be constantly endured because he is "disturbed by a thousand fancies, and his pride shows him even in his dreams those fancied pleasures; he is tormented by a desire which will never be satisfied."[82] Long before distinguished psychiatrists such as Alfred Adler dreamed of the inferiority complex, or Freud thought of the theory of wish-fulfillment of dreams, Rousseau was explicating these profound and lasting psychological truths.

By contrast to this troubled youth, Rousseau's adolescent pupil is happy merely in noting how many ills he has escaped. Of his own free will he shares the sufferings of his fellow creatures, and even finds pleasure in so doing. "He enjoys at once the pity he feels for their woes and the joy of being exempt from them. ... To pity another's woes we must indeed know them, but we need not feel them."[83] Once having suffered, a person always fears repetition and hence pities those enduring suffering. "A hard-hearted man is always unhappy, since the state of his heart leaves him no superfluous sensibility to bestow on the sufferings of others."[84] Happiness should not be judged merely by appearances; mirth is not an index of happiness since a person manifesting merriment can well be a wretch attempting to deceive others and distract himself. As a rule those seemingly jovial, friendly, contented people at their clubs are usually the gloomy grumblers at home. How well Rousseau understood the modern psychological mechanism of compensation! "The man of the world almost always wears a mask. He is scarcely ever himself and is almost a stranger to himself; he is ill at ease when he is forced into his own company."[85] Anyone who carefully examines his own life will discover that moderate enjoyment produces the pleasantest habit of mind, a felicitous state of mind which eclipses desire and aversion. "The unrest of passion causes curiosity and fickleness; the emptiness of noisy pleasures causes weariness. We never weary of our state when we know none more delightful."[86] The pupil's character will be softened and mellowed if he is given some acquaintance or experience with human misery.

Emile has now reached the stage of moral discrimination, in which the first step has been to control his passions and pleasures. A second step toward manhood is essential. It is time for the heart's sensitivity and his true affections to be enlightened by reason, with justice and kindness becoming more than mere abstractions. Heretofore Emile has thought only of himself. He must henceforth study society, politics, and morals, all of them so intertwined that it is impossible to study the one without considering the others. He must also study historical facts, not those having undergone a transformation in the mind of the historian, the worst historians being those rendering opinions. "Facts! Facts! and let him decide for himself; this is how he will learn to know mankind."[87] Modern history, lacking character, is relegated to one side because its people are all alike. Preference should be given to reading about the lives of outstanding individuals because that provides the best insight into the human heart. A proper study of men would entail "a great wish to know men, great impartiality of judgment, a heart sufficiently sensitive to understand every human passion, and calm enough to be free from passion."[88]

Any sane person will find any folly remedial but folly itself. Emile, a lover of peace, does not take to noise or quarrelling, even among animals. Consequently dog fights and animal suffering, rather than pleasing him, cause him to suffer sympathetically. It is the extension of the love of justice that brings about the love of the human race. He has learned the first concern of the wise man, viz., the promotion of the general well-being or happiness of all.

To prevent pity degenerating into weakness we must generalise it and extend it to mankind. Then we only yield to it when it is in accordance with justice, since justice is of all the virtues that which contributes most to the common good. Reason and self-love compel us to love mankind even more than our neighbor.[89]

Rousseau's objective is to develop Emile into a rational man who will not be swayed by passions and prejudices but only by reason. Such a person, being a natural man, sees with his eyes and feels with his heart, but he is not a savage.

Rousseau never wearies of summoning his readers: "Let all the lessons of young people take the form of doing rather than talking; let them learn nothing from books which they can learn from experience."[90] The same dictum holds true for instruction in religion. At fifteen years of age Emile will be unaware that he possesses a soul, and may not be prepared to learn about it at the age of eighteen. If religious dogmas comprise mysteries beyond the understanding of adults, why trouble children with what they cannot understand? "Let us beware of proclaiming the truth to those who cannot as yet comprehend it, for to do so is to try to inculcate error."[91] The way to teach religion to a child is for the parents never to discuss theoretical issues of religion, but merely to mention the name of God intermittently in conversations with utmost reverence and devotion. Thus the child's curiosity and self-love will be stimulated so that he will look forward to learning about religion with anticipation and appreciation. *The Creed of the Vicar of Savoy,* a discussion in the fourth book of the *Emile,* sets forth Rousseau's *natural religion*—a deism! Revelation for the deist derives from the "spectacle of nature," from conscience, and from reason.

Emile is now a young man. Having reached the "last act of youth's drama," it is undesirable that he remain alone. Accordingly a helpmate must be found for him—Sophie. (See Chapter VI.)

VII *Principles of the* Emile *Applied to the Education of a Boy*

Rousseau's correspondence with Abbé M. in 1770 dealt with the education of a boy of high rank along the lines prescribed by and adapted from the *Emile.* The record of the boy's rearing indicates that he has strayed from nature and that his social atmosphere has contributed to his poor development. "Once there has been a departure from the straight path of nature, nothing is more difficult than to return to it."[92] Ordinarily the bad habits acquired during the first and last stages of childhood are the least difficult to eradicate, but an objective, rational remedy is required. The human mind is moved by reason, sentiment, and necessity, an important lesson of life for one to learn being to "bend to the yoke of necessity."

A boy of the age of this one has accumulated prejudices, as, for example, his attitude of regarding his father as a hired hand subject to his capricious whims. He must learn that birth and riches are not of greatest worth; his vain soul must bow before virtue; and he must achieve respect for justice and courage. The boy requires a model for the cultivation of virtues, and the father should be that model. To make a man of him is to do the work of God; education is a divine endeavor to be undertaken only by a man of virtue, a virtue that cannot be feigned. It is necessary to command respect—even by force. It is preferable to have an unhappy child than a contemptible man. Punishment should not degenerate into physical violence, but should entail deprivation, the extent thereof depending upon the offence. Attachment and good will are the most effective ways of influencing a strong mind. Kindness is essential in taming a lion or a boy. Fundamentally the objective is to win his love. If you succeed in that, he will "walk on red-hot irons" for you.

Rousseau was not dogmatic or adamant about his philosophical position, for he insisted only upon the correct interpretation and application of his basic principles. He expected some of his recommendations would be subject to modification in the light of particular situations, but he called for the consistent and systematic application of his philosophy of education, and he asserted that such application requires three personality traits: vigilance, patience, and firmness—three qualities that cannot be relaxed for even a moment. To educate a child successfully is to bestow on mankind a gift, to find self-satisfaction, and to acquire a friend, for respect, esteem, and gratitude will have been ingrained in the pupil. A decade of education invested with unremitting toil will produce satisfying dividends of lifelong pleasure.

VIII *Lasting Pedagogical Values of the* Emile

The fact that many of Rousseau's proposals seem commonplace today attests to their permanent value. The excitement his ideas generated when first expounded served education well. Commonplace as they now are, it took a Rousseau to remind the pedagogues of his day of their importance. Although the ideal of physical development was as old as Plato's philosophy of education, it had become a lost part of educational theory and practice. Since a healthy body and a healthy mind are closely interrelated, Rousseau wanted the athlete's rigor to be combined with the sage's reason so that men would learn to work like peasants but think like philosophers.

Rousseau advocated education in open country because of its fresh air, the opportunities for freedom of movement and physical exercise, and a natural environment which develops courage and other virtues.

He stressed the utilitarian value of learning a trade, of being apprenticed in some manual vocation. Should adversity strike, one could fall back upon his trade as a source of financial security. He anticipated the Puritan ethic in his statement that, rich or poor, everyone should work, for only a cheat does not work.

Rousseau also emphasized the necessity for training the senses. It had been Locke's thesis that there is nothing in the mind which was not first in the senses, a thesis which Condillac accepted and which in turn was passed on by both philosophers to Rousseau who felt that, inasmuch as the senses are the first to be formed, they should be the first to be cultivated. The child's education should not consist of explanations but of experience with things, for education is to be both utilitarian and a process involving the handling of tangible objects.

The program of education should be directed principally toward real preparation for life by present living, not by abstractions, not geared to the study of history and literature, but to the development and guidance of physical and moral energy. Education must be adapted to life instead of aiming at the storage of facts in a memory bank. The ultimate goal of education is to produce a person who is more teachable than taught, not a scholar but a person with a taste and thirst for knowledge. Instead of becoming a sort of computerized mechanical storehouse of memorized information, the pupil should be taught constructive predispositions, a desire for original discovery, competence in doing his own research, individual effort, and ways to enlarge his knowledge as he develops the necessary aptitude for its acquisition. The ability to do things well, to become fit for the actual business of life, is vital. Geography, astronomy, and physics will not be taught from maps and books, but from nature walks, excursions, and careful observation of natural phenomena. Grammar will be mastered by noting its correct usage in the language of mother and teacher. Thus basic education depends essentially upon the will more than the intellect, and the pupil acquires it by means of emancipation and self-direction in enjoyable activity. The child's task must never become irksome, for if it does, whatever he learns will be of no account. Be not beguiled, said Rousseau, for good men are to be preferred to scholars.

The well-taught person knows how to cope with suffering, and his carefully cultivated social feelings contribute to his spirit of philanthropy. The education of skilled people for the professions is not of the essence; the aim of forming "just a man" is fundamental. Rousseau's philosophy of education proclaimed children's rights, their right to a liberated education. His *Emile* is still the child's charter of freedom and the most influential guide to democratic education.

CHAPTER 6

Emile (Book V)—Sophie: Education of an Ideal Woman

Having articulated his philosophy for educating the perfect man, Rousseau turned his attention in the fifth book of *Emile* to the philosophy of educating the ideal woman. At the time Rousseau was a guest of the Duchess of Luxembourg in Montmorency. Sophie, Rousseau's ideal woman, actually existed though she is to a great extent the product of his imagination. Her education, the counterpart and opposite of Emile's, calls for her education by nature, but the female nature is inferior to the male's, for the sexes are not equal. She possesses qualities peculiar to the female. Her education, a limited one, is geared for housework and needlework, with religious instruction to appear in due season. She requires common sense in order to cope with duties of wife and mother, for these are her natural calling, not to be cloistered and wasted in a convent. Modern, attractive, and with natural graces, she should enter society.

Sophie, as much a woman as Emile is a man, is to be educated to assume her place in the physical and moral order as well as being Emile's helpmate. Except for her female sexual organs she is like a man in the sense that she possesses the same faculties and needs. However, nature made her subservient to the male. "The man should be strong and active; the woman should be weak and passive.... Woman is specially made for man's delight."[1] Thus woman is expected to please man as well as being in subjection to him.

Although endowed with limitless passion, women possess an innate modesty enabling them to restrain themselves and to stir a man's passion. Nature also decreed that woman shall reign, for "the stronger party seems to be master, but is as a matter of fact dependent on the weaker. . .by an inexorable law of nature."[2] While man is only intermittently a male, the female is invariably a female, with everything reminding her of her sex. Patience and gentleness keynote her education.

The seeming inequality of man-made law is dictated by reason, not by any desire to be unfair. Her proper business is bearing children, hence her greatest crime is infidelity because she has robbed her husband of his rightful inheritance—his own child. She must be more than faithful; her reputation must be impeccable.

I *Importance of Femininity in Women*

Women must be cultivated to be feminine, "for woman is worth more as a woman and less as a man. . . . To cultivate the masculine virtues in women and to neglect their own is evidently to do them an injury. . . . Do not try to make your daughter a good man in defiance of nature."[3] A manly woman rather than gaining power forfeits her reign over men. "The more women are like men, the less influence they will have over men, and then men will be masters indeed."[4] Whereas the man depends on the woman because of his desire, the woman depends on the man because of her needs as well as her desires. Nature decrees that a woman must bow to a man's judgment.

The early education of a girl stresses physical training, for the body's birth precedes that of the mind, and consequently its cultivation comes first. While the physical training of boys is for the purpose of developing strength, the aim for girls is grace. These qualities are not peculiar to sex, but the simple fact is that "women should be strong enough to do anything gracefully; men should be skillful enough to do anything easily."[5] To exaggerate delicacy in women contributes to effeminacy in men. Rousseau believed that both reason and nature dictate that women's place is in the home. "Everything that cramps and confines nature is in bad taste,"[6] hence overadorning the female with jewelry detracts from her natural beauty.

Games should be coeducational because when children mature the games played as adults include both sexes. As children, however, their games instinctively tend toward their life's calling, the girl with her dolls and the boys in competitive sports. Both sexes possess good sense and should attend only to useful studies. Although both boys and girls should be subject to authority, girls should be more so, for when a girl marries she will have to submit to the authority of her spouse. Neither boys nor girls should be required to read; life will begin her arithmetic lessons the very first time she makes an error in counting. "If the little girl does not get the cherries for her lunch without an arithmetical exercise, she will soon learn to count."[7] Her greatest lesson, one in self-control, guarantees against dissipation, frivolity, and inconstancy. Society being what it is, "the life of a good woman is a perpetual struggle against self."[8]

If a child does not find delight in her mother's company, she probably will not turn out well. To obviate this problem, mother and daughter should be in constant communication, with unceasing care, and habit itself will do the rest. "Habit is all that is needed, as you have nature on your side."[9] The most desired quality in a woman is gentleness. Ironically this gentle person "should early learn to submit to injustice and to suffer the wrongs inflicted on her by her husband without complaint."[10] The trait of gentleness is primarily for her own benefit, ameliorating the effect of the misdeeds suffered at her husband's hands. "Heaven did not make women attractive and persuasive that they might degenerate into bitterness, or meek that they should desire the mastery; their soft voice was not meant for hard words."[11]

Every natural inclination is right, every natural law good. The female with her feminine traits and her wit as a ready resource can easily reign over the man. Devoid of these characteristics she would be man's slave instead of his helpmeet. Thus it is important to "educate your women as women."[12] A young girl should not act like an old woman, but be merry, eager, and lively, singing and dancing to her heart's content, and enjoying every pleasure of youth.

Women have ready tongues; they talk earlier, more easily, and more pleasantly than men. . . . A man says what he knows, a woman says what will please; the one needs knowledge, the other taste; utility should be the man's object; the woman speaks to give pleasure. There should be nothing in common but truth.[13]

While a man's politeness is more helpful, the woman's is more caressing.

II *Religious Education*

Public opinion governs a woman's conduct, and authority her religion. A daughter follows her mother's religion, the wife her husband's. When administering religious instruction to little girls (which is permissable for them but not for boys), it should not be gloomy, tiresome, a duty, a task, or something committed to memory. Teach by example. "Example! Example! Without it you will never succeed in teaching children anything."[14] Permit them to hear you praying, but keep your prayers brief, reverent, and respectful.

The child's answers should not be given to her by means of catechism or drilling, but spontaneous ones which she sincerely thinks and believes. Otherwise, the child's answers, if she does not understand them, will be lies, for she will be expected to affirm that which she cannot believe.

The first question I find in our catechism is as follows: "Who created you and brought you into the world?" To which the girl, who thinks it was her mother, replies without hesitation, "It was God." All she knows is that she is asked a question which she only half understands and she gives an answer she does not understand at all.[15]

Rousseau contended that a Socratic approach should be employed in answering the same question after the following manner which he considered to be a method of teaching by means of concrete examples:

Tutor:
Do you remember when your mother was a little girl?
Girl:
No.
Why not, when you have such a good memory?
I was not alive.
Then you were not always alive!
No.
Will you live for ever?
Yes.
Are you young or old?
I am young.
Is your grandmamma old or young?
She is old.
Was she ever young?
Yes.
Why is she not young now?
She has grown old.
Will you grow old, too?
I don't know.
Where are your last year's frocks?
They have not been chosen.
Why?
Because they were too small for me.
Why were they too small?
I have grown bigger.
Will you grow any more?
Oh, yes.
And what becomes of big girls?
They grow into women.
And what becomes of women?
They are mothers.
And what becomes of mothers?
They grow old.
Will you grow old?
When I am a mother.
And what becomes of old people?
I don't know.
What became of your grandfather?
He died.
Why did he die?
Because he was old.
What becomes of old people?
They die.

And when you are old—?
Oh, I don't want to die!
My dear, no one wants to die, and everybody dies.
Why,.will mamma die too?
Yes, like everybody else. Women grow old as well as men, and old age ends in death.
What must I do to grow old very, very slowly?
Be good while you are little.
I will always be good.
So much the better. But do you suppose you will live for ever?
When I am very, very old—
Well?
When we are so very old you say we must die?
You must die some day.
Oh, dear! I suppose I must.
Who lived before you?
My father and mother.
And before them?
Their father and mother.
Who will live after you?
My children.
Who will live after them?
Their children.[16]

By this Socratic technique (though Rousseau does not refer to it as such), each of the difficult metaphysical questions pertaining to religion can be tackled. Otherwise, religious doctrines will be just so many words without ideas. The method of education may be changed when the girl reaches an age when she can make her own judgments, "the age when the reason becomes enlightened, when growing emotion gives a voice to conscience."[17] The two factors governing a woman are public opinion and her individual conscience.

III *Sophie's Character*

Sophie is a well-born woman of good disposition with a warm heart, keen mind, and pleasant temper, with an imagination by which she is occasionally carried away. While some women possess her good qualities and others even have excellent traits lacking in her, "in no one are these qualities better blended to form a happy disposition."[18] One may be indifferent on encountering Sophie, but no one when leaving her will be able to do so without warm feelings.

Though not beautiful, in fact barely pretty, Sophie becomes prettier the more one is with her. "She does not dazzle; she arouses interest; she delights us, we know not why."[19] Her graceful figure, however, excels all. Her natural gifts includes a pretty voice which she uses to sing tastefully. She possesses more taste than talent, stepping along lightly and gracefully.

While Sophie is fond of dress, knowing how to dress well, her tastes are simple but elegant, becoming but not showy. She favors needlework but enjoys other feminine arts, except for cooking and "kitchen" gardening because she does not care to soil herself, a consequence of her mother's teaching with respect to personal cleanliness being an important responsibility of a lady. By nature she is fond of good things. Once she was temperate by habit, whereas now she is temperate by virtue. Though she likes and appreciates good home-made dishes, she is desirous of maintaining her fine figure and therefore eats sparingly.

Sophie's personality includes a naturally merry temperament, with a modest and retiring disposition. Her conversations are attractive and her mind pleasing but not brilliant, thorough but not profound. Her sensitive nature does not permit her always to be good humored, and her gentleness does not allow her to be disagreeable in company. If hurt, she will leave, and with her heart swelling, cry. Tears are an effective device women have over men. A gentle and submissive personality, she has the talent of making one forget her wrongdoing and even think that it is a virtue. She makes amends unfailingly, and is ashamed of the fault more than the punishment. While eager to atone for her own wrongdoing, she patiently endures wrongs done her.

In accordance with a simple and reasonable religion consisting of few doctrines and still fewer observances, Sophie's life is devoted to doing good and service to God. She, with reverent submission, has accepted her parental instruction with respect to religion which she acquired from them by their example, the example being engraved on her heart. Sophie, who loves virtue as a ruling passion, knows that vir-

tue is "the only road to real happiness. She finds nothing
fairer in itself than virtue and regards it as a woman's glory.
Preferring to give pleasure rather than attract attention,
Sophie, who has a consuming desire for love, prefers to "give
pleasure to one good man than be a general favorite. . . . She
wants a lover, not a circle of admirers."[20] Having been
taught the rights and duties of both sexes, Sophie entertains
the highest ideal of virtue of womanhood. "But she would
rather think of a virtuous man, a man of true worth; she
knows that she is made for such a man, that she is worthy of
him, that she can make him as happy as he will make
her."[21] Although she possesses a feminine desire to please,
she has but little knowledge of society. Sophie, whose opinion of the rights of women is quite high, assumes a respectful attitude toward members of her own sex.

IV *Selection of a Husband for Sophie*

At fifteen years of age Sophie is no longer a child inasmuch as her matured judgment is comparable to that of a
woman of twenty. The choice of a husband, unlike the prevailing custom, remains her option. Knowing how a married
couple can live happily in poverty, she recognizes their first
duty as loving each other. "Sophie has only a good disposition and an ordinary heart; her education is responsible for
everything in which she excels other women."[22] Sophie has
been trained as a helpmate for Emile, both being educated
for each other.

A happy marriage calls for stifling prejudices, forgetting
human or social institutions, and consulting nature. Women,
possessing a natural gift for the management of men, rule
over them with gentleness, tact, and kindness, their caresses
being their commands, their tears being their threats.

Since man by nature thinks but seldom, he must acquire
such skills with great difficulty during his acquisition of the
arts. However, a thinking man should select only a woman
who thinks as his mate, just as an educated man should
choose a woman who is educated. Beauty, unlike education,
is not desirable in a woman, for its dangers last while its
appreciation is but of short duration. "Unless a beautiful

woman is an angel, her husband is the most miserable of men; and even if she were an angel he would still be the center of a hostile crowd and she could not prevent it."[23] Actually extreme ugliness is preferable to extreme beauty if it were at all tolerable. "Desire mediocrity in all things, even in beauty."[24] A man should love and serve his spouse, not with foolish fleeting passion, but with lasting attention to settled principles engraved upon his heart so that, when buffeted by fortune, his adoration of her will remain unshaken.

V *Education of Sophie of Wirtemberg*

Emile was published in 1752, and during that decade its proposed system of education was praised throughout Europe as a paradigm for educating children. Rousseau was sought out by prominent people for pedagogical advice. One such person who solicited Rousseau's assistance was Prince Louis Eugène of Wirtemberg, who corresponded with him about the education of an infant daughter, Sophie. Winning the Prince of Wirtemberg as a disciple helped to convert other noblemen willing to replace court pomposity with natural simplicity in their educational programs, at least to the extent possible for royal families under prevailing circumstances.

Rousseau, who deemed it a misfortune for anyone to be princely born while remaining enslaved to the artificiality of such a station and its conventions, feared that it might be still worse for royal fathers who attempted to cope with the obstacles posed by their rank when undertaking to educate a child according to nature so that he would become a properly educated human being. Compromise seemed to be the only possible solution.

Emphasizing the important fact that only a father is capable of offering fatherly care, and that only a mother could provide a mother's care, Rousseau formulated the following three rules for parents of high station in life whose official duties prevent them from devoting their own time to the child's care. (1) Make sure that your child is dear to the governess. (2) The governess must have her line of action all marked out for her, and she must have perfect confidence in

its success. (3) The governess ought to be given absolute
control over the child.[25]

(1) For the sake of the first rule, the governess should be
of the same sex as the pupil, preferably not a young or
beautiful woman, for the young women have preoccupations
that can be distracting and the beautiful ones will be interrupted by numerous admirers. A widow is preferable to a
girl who has never married, but her own children should not
be with her. A clever woman, despite lofty sentiments, is
undesirable, and the same is true of a lightheaded one and
one who is too easygoing. The governess must have good
practical judgment, but she need not be a cultured person;
in fact, so much the better if she is illiterate, for then she
can learn side by side with her pupil.

Amusing the child will not win love for the governess; affection, if it is not forthcoming from spontaneous sentiment,
will develop out of self-interest. Intertwining the lot of the
governess with that of the child tends to make the child
dear to the governess. Not mere service per se, but successful service, is what counts. Consequently the rewards for the
governess must be commensurate with successful services
rendered; any father endowed with probity and discernment
will be able to determine justly the degree of her success. In
the absence of the father, however, the mother's judgment
will not suffice, inasmuch as a mother's love is blind, with
the result that the governess will only seek to please the
mother instead of devoting herself to the proper rearing of
the child.

The father may reason with the governess to motivate
her, but the effect of such an appeal will be slight, and the
same is true of any appeal to her self-interest unless she has
real imagination enough to see the remote consequences of
her work upon her future career. What is required is a person of deep feeling, for which a lively imagination is necessary. The offer of monetary rewards can be useful, but not if
they are deferred to a remote future.

A strict governess will win the love of her pupil, provided
that the child has not been spoiled and she maintains adequate discipline from the start. If the child begins with definite, natural, good habits, they will have a positive effect un-

less counteracted by the unwise interference of outsiders. The governess will do justice to the child and will not sit by complacently, for such an attitude makes children discontented and too demanding. The child who loves her teacher knows that the teacher's success depends upon her pupil's achievements.

(2) In order to fulfill the second rule, it is necessary to provide the teacher with a memoir of instructions, which she should commit to memory. As the father's representative, she will carry out her orders faithfully without expecting to be furnished with reasons for them. The memoir should specify the goals of instruction—the mental and physical development which the pupil is expected to attain. All the teacher needs to understand is the feasibility of the plan and the techniques to be utilized for its execution. She may discuss with the parents the pedagogical programs but not alter them, and thereby should become convinced as to the validity of the recommended instructional methods. The child's mother will understand the principles underlying the memoir of instructions, but the teacher need only know the rules governing the procedures of instruction.

(3) In order to fulfill the third rule, the memoir must be strictly implemented in all things. Full compliance with the memoir will achieve co-operative action and mutual understanding among the parties. The memoir must be explained to the teacher and other employees, not in terms of philosophy but as a matter of morality and piety.

CHAPTER 7

The Influence of Rousseau

Rousseau's influence has been pervasive throughout the Western world, profoundly affecting the ideas of philosophers and educators and the political as well as the educational institutions of Europe and America. His two most influential works were undoubtedly *The Social Contract,* the ideas of which were among the most important foundations of the French Revolution and the American Declaration of Independence; and *Emile,* which stimulated a comparable revolution in educational theory and, eventually, educational practice among democratic nations.

I *Rousseau's Influence in Europe*

In France religious leaders severely attacked Rousseau; nevertheless, soon after the Revolution, the government responded to public demand with limited reorganization of the schools. In England his writings were translated and widely read, but his influence was not immediately substantial since that country had no national system of education. In Germany, however, *Emile* was extraordinarily influential, with growing movements promoting naturalism and freedom as key principles of education. The character of Julie also caught the imagination of the people, giving women added self-respect and men an appreciation of the dignity of women.

118

The French reacted with "impish merriment" to Rousseau's brilliance and Julie's saintliness. From 1760 to the time of the Revolution, the hysteria of women over Rousseau reached such a pitch that they were prepared to purchase at any price some memento of their genius, such as a glass out of which he drank, or be ready to kiss any paper containing his handwriting. Women vowed to consecrate their lives to him if he would only accept their offer as a token of gratitude. Unable to cope with the demand for his books, French merchants resorted to renting out books by Rousseau with an hour's limit on each volume. Intoxication with his publications spread like a contagious epidemic among all classes—lawyers, soldiers, entrepreneurs, and courtiers alike. Musset-Pathay related one story about a lady, dressed in her finery to attend a ball, who planned to read one of Rousseau's books for about a half-hour but found herself still reading at midnight with her carriage still waiting. When the matter was called to her attention, she was too engrossed in reading to reply and continued reading until four in the morning when she undressed for bed but instead of going to sleep read the entire night through. Many comparable stories about the reactions of other genteel women were told. Yet resistance of the Church and of aristocrats limited the extent of educational reforms, some of which, in fact, were eventually reversed by reactionary governments.

The extraordinary excitement in France had its counterpart in Germany, where the sentimental movement for Rousseau's naturalism even produced such groups as the Order of Sentiment, the Order of Mercy and Expiation, and other pseudoreligious associations. In contrast to the situation in England, Rousseau's influence in Germany was spectacular. Schiller was so enamored with Rousseau's works that he saw him as the apostle who "converted Christians into human beings." He crowned Rousseau as a Socrates who sought to make men of Christians. In his poem, "Rousseau," he wrote:

As Socrates by sophists was brought low,
So Christians tortured, Christians felled Rousseau—
Rousseau, who called on Christians to be men.[1]

In Schiller's mind Rousseau had become a martyr. Lessing declared: "The name Rousseau cannot be uttered without respect." The younger generation in Germany (like the youth of France) advocated the return to nature. Important German writers were discussing Rousseau and incorporating his philosophy into their own works.

The German educational reformer Johann Bernhard Basedow (1724-1790) founded in 1774 a model school, the Philanthropinum, which implemented Rousseau's theories with intense enthusiasm. (Basedow, since he had no son, named his daughter Emilie.) The famous Swiss educational reformer Johann Heinrich Pestalozzi (1746-1827) put into practice the educational theories of *Emile* in a school that he established for poor children on his own estate at Neuhof. Notwithstanding this school's failure in 1780, he derived constructive principles of education from the experiment and became Rousseau's successor in educational reform. Rousseau's influence, through Pestalozzi, spread not only in Germany but throughout Europe and in America. An ardent disciple of Rousseau, Friedrich Froebel (1782-1852), eager to supplant books with things as a means of instruction and to spark the spontaneity of children, founded the kindergarten movement in Germany. This student of Pestalozzi established a kindergarten school for children between the ages of three and seven years which became a model for kindergartens throughout Germany.

The classical German philosopher Kant, who declared that no book had moved him as deeply as had *Emile,* was so greatly influenced by Rousseau's writings that he changed his attitude toward the masses from one of disdain to one of wholesome respect. Kant, whose daily walks were carried out with minute regularity and precision, was disturbed because he could not pull himself away from reading *Emile.* It inspired him to write his own famous treatise on education, which included many ideas generated by the *Emile.* In addition to accepting Rousseau's basic premise that nature is good, he introduced his own version of the rights of man, asserting that every man is to be regarded as an end in himself; furthermore, his insistence on freedom (the existence of an autonomous and inalienable will in children as in adults) was inspired by Rousseau's demand that no person should be subjected to the will of another. Even Kant's distinction between moral and physical punishment owes much to Rousseau. Kant wrote: "Punishment is either *physical* or *moral*. It is *moral* when we do something derogatory to the child's longing to be honoured and loved (a longing which is an aid to moral training); for instance, when we humiliate the child by treating him coldly and distantly."[2]

Another German writer, Jean Paul Friedrich Richter (1762-1825), a tutor near Hof, wrote a classic volume on pedagogy (*Levana*) in 1807 in which he voiced his indebtedness to *Emile,* calling it an incomparable work without precedent.

The fantastic reaction *Emile* incited toward the end of the eighteenth century throughout Europe was almost incredible, for a wide variety of Emiles made their appearance, including Christian Emiles, new Emiles, anti-Emiles, corrected Emiles, retouched Emiles, Emiles adapted to social life, improved Emiles, and amplified Emiles. Not only were children being reared a là Emile, but even the dress fashions of the day were designed "in the Jean-Jacques style."

II *Influence of Rousseau in America*

The writing of Rousseau lent spirit to both the French and the American revolutions. Jefferson was profoundly influenced by Rousseau's appeal in behalf of man's inalienable rights to life, liberty, and the pursuit of happiness when he wrote the Declaration of Independence. Thomas Paine fell strongly under the same influence. Rousseau's pen made of him one of the foremost revolutionaries of all times and a potent precursor of the American Revolution. Although Rousseau was known in America as early as 1751, it was not until 1789 that serious preoccupation with his ideas spread among the masses of people and, in 1790, one of his books enjoyed a brisk library circulation. The last decade of the eighteenth century saw three publishers in the United States issuing editions of his works, including *Julie, or the New Heloise; The Confessions; The Social Contract;* and *Discourse on Political Economy.* Owing to *The Confessions,* his image was damaged in the Colonies, yet many readers still esteemed him highly. The very fact that his books were published at all in early America was a singular honor.

His repute as a writer was well known to the literary giants of America, with Jefferson noting his eminence and William Ellery Channing praising *Julie, or the New Heloise,* which became a best seller in the United States before the close of the eighteenth century, rivalling such classics as Shakespeare's plays and *Gulliver's Travels.* In his *Rousseau in America 1760-1809,* Spurlin remarked: "Books of Rousseau were in the libraries of statesmen and clergymen, law professors and judges, teachers, essayists and editors, and men in other walks of life."[3]

However, Rousseau also had his enemies in the United States, especially John Adams who disparaged his philosophy as "a mass of nonsense and inconsistency." Like John Adams before him, Noah Webster, who had previously been attracted by Rousseau's writings, later condemned them on the ground of their "artificial reasoning."

Both the *New Heloise* and the *Emile* were held in suspicion as insidious in character and were the chief sources of fear and distrust of Rousseau. The *New Heloise* was regarded as promoting immorality, while the *Emile* raised the specter of deism in the minds of clergymen, editors (especially editors of religious journals), and members of other professions. Although opinion about him was just about evenly divided, his antagonists were more vociferous than his sympathizers. "All in all," wrote Spurlin, "and excepting the conclusions as regards *The New Eloisa* and the support given religion by the *Emile,* it is obvious that Rousseau had vogue but not influence in eighteenth-century America."[4] Ironically the principal immediate influence of *Emile* was in religion.

As for *Julie, or the New Heloise* which Rousseau himself regarded as a novel meant especially for women, rather than as a philosophical discourse, this milestone of epistolary fiction emerged as a best seller soon after publication. The book, available in English during the year of its publication, was advertised in America the following year (1862) by D. Hall, and was soon being sold by booksellers from Boston to Williamsburg, with even George Washington having a copy in his library.

CHAPTER 8

Critical Reactions to Rousseau's Philosophy

There has been no dearth of critics of Rousseau's philosophy. For over two centuries he has been lauded and attacked. He was undoubtedly one of the greatest philosophers of all time; he was without a peer among French (and Swiss) political and educational philosophers. By democratic multitudes he was loved, by conservatives and aristocrats hated, for being the author who more than any other inspired the French Revolution.

His influence extends beyond educational and political philosophy to the fields of art and literature, in both of which fields some regard him as having sired the romantic movement. It has rightfully been said that modern educational theory stems from his writings, certainly at least its inspiration; but it must not be forgotten that John Locke's treatise on education antedated the writings of Rousseau and provided Rousseau with the impetus that he needed both for writing about and for concentrating his attention on problems of education.

I *Remarks of John Morley*

John Morley was an eminent scholar with a special interest in Rousseau's works. His notable two-volume study,

Rousseau, was published in 1873. He commented that although the opening words of Rousseau's *The Social Contract,* "Man is born free, and everywhere he is in chains," had the effect of sending "such a thrill through the generation to which they were uttered in two continents,"[1] Rousseau failed to inform his readers that earlier civilizations were not free, were actually not as well off. How is man born free? "If he is born into isolation, he perishes instantly. If he is born into a family, he is at the moment of his birth committed to a state of social relation, in however rudimentary a form; and the more or less of freedom which this state may ultimately permit to him, depends upon circumstances."[2] What freedom was there for the Athenian or Roman child who was subject to death by exposure at birth? What freedom was there for the sons of the ancient Hebrew patriarchs, such as the son of Abraham whose life was subject to sacrifice? Yet Rousseau held the Judaic law in high regard.

Morley protested against the disregard for authority in Rousseau's educational philosophy, and viewed this position as a fundamental weakness in his system. "One of the most important of educating influences is lost, if the young are not taught to place the feelings of others in a front place, when they think in their own simple way of what will happen to them, if they yield to a given impulse. Rousseau was quite right in insisting on practical experiences of consequences as the only secure foundation for self-acting habit; he was fatally wrong in mutilating this experience by the exclusion from it of the effect of perceiving, resisting, accepting, ignoring, all will and authority from without."[3] Morley held that children will develop many excellent qualities if they learn to respect fully informed authorities.

Although he found Rousseau's concept of justice generally valid, Morley criticized the lack of adequate explanation or elaboration. Rousseau spoke of justice as "the love of the human race," and asserted that "of all the virtues, justice is that which contributes most to the common good of men." These high-sounding ideas are quite appealing, but Morley complained: "What constitutes justice, what is its standard, what its source, what its sanction, whence the extraordinary holiness with which its name has come to be invested among the most highly civilized societies of men, we are never told, nor do we ever see that our teacher has seen the possibility of such questions being asked."⁴ How Rousseau would handle these questions is difficult to say, but Morley speculated that he would perhaps have taken refuge in the convenient mystery of the natural law, a term which in Rousseau's time implied a state of perfect human relations.

Morley contrasted Rousseau's view of Emile's education with his biased attitude toward the education of women. The education of Emile was designed first and foremost to make him a natural man, for that was to be his real calling, and only secondarily was he to become a soldier, merchant, physician, or the like. The great educator who saw clearly the errors of civilization from which men must be protected had absorbed the widespread prejudice of the contemporary society against women. Instead of portraying his ideal woman, Sophie, as a human being with interests, reason, emotions, he restricted her primarily to the role of wife and house-mother.

Rousseau's view of women was both oriental and obscurantist; they were never to be allowed a free mind of their own but were to remain subservient to their husbands. The purpose of their training was to teach them patience and endurance—to accustom them to being thwarted and restrained—because such virtues would be necessary for them in marriage. If they attempted to free themselves from this unfortunate requirement of their sex, they would only subject themselves to more severe ordeals. While the male child was to be instructed in religion beginning at the age of fifteen years, a girl would have to adopt the religious beliefs prescribed by her husband, for she could never acquire the mental capacity to cope with problems of religion. Morley severely condemned Rousseau's bold assertion that woman was created in order to yield to her male companion and suffer his injustices. It may be a fact, he said, that women suffer the injustices of men, but to view this as the divine plan is to indulge in intellectual recklessness.

Morley pointed out that Rousseau acknowledged the superior native intelligence of women, but then required women to be observers while men were to be the thinkers.

"It is rather like a mockery to end the matter by a fervid assurance, that in spite of prejudices that have their origin in the manners of the time, the enthusiasm for what is worthy and noble is no more foreign to women than it is to men, and that there is nothing which under the guidance of nature may not be obtained from them as well as from ourselves."[5] To make the matter even more obscure and contradictory, Rousseau confesses to only two truly distinct classes: people who think and those who do not think. After admitting that the difference is due to education and may relate to either sex, he advises the thinkers to intermarry, for a male who is a thinker should not be compelled to think in solitude. How is a woman to become a thinker, Morley asked, if her educational life is geared for mental bondage? He attributed Rousseau's ensnarement by such "pernicious nonsense" mainly to the fact that he lacked a "conception of improvement in human affairs." If he had had an adequate conception of social progress, he would have realized that any major educational reform would have to include an acknowledgment of women's capacities as one of the first steps toward improvement. According to Morley, moreover, the fifth book of *Emile,* the portion devoted to female education, is really an idyll, not a serious treatment of the problems involved in the education of girls. If Rousseau meant it as a serious contribution to the philosophy of education, it is worthless as such, but "as an idyll it is delicious; as a serious contribution to the hardest of problems it is naught."[6] Yet the book does have considerable merit derived from the romantic spirit animating it and communicating itself vividly to the reader.

It was Morley's opinion that Rousseau had simply invented the ideal state of nature and had erred in repudiating history and experience, for evidence from these sources provides the grounds on which to construct a valid and viable theory of social change.

His narrow, symmetrical, impatient humour unfitted him to deal with the complex tangle of the history of social growths. It was essential to his mental comfort that he should be able to see a picture of perfect order and logical system at both ends of his speculation.

Hence, he invented, to begin with, his ideal state of nature, and an ideal mode of passing from that to the social state.[7]

Rousseau's virtual ignorance of history explains why he selected a few facts gleaned from his scanty perusal of historical literature as the basis for his condemnation of history. Lack of knowledge of the historical method led him astray.

Furthermore, according to Morley, the writings of Rousseau are charged with inflammatory dogmas that germinate fanatic sects. Disciplined reasoning and careful examination of data and proofs are too often neglected.

Let us here remark that it was exactly what strikes us as the desperate absurdity of the assumptions of *The Social Contract,* which constituted the power of that work, when it accidentally fell into the hands of men who surveyed a national system wrecked in all its parts. *The Social Contract* is worked out precisely in that fashion which, if it touches men at all, makes them into fanatics.[8]

There are those persons who cannot cope with a carefully worked out and developed principle, but find a vigorously compact system irresistible; these are the individuals who come to the forefront for a time in periods of distraction when they calculate that it is the best opportunity for seizing power.

Morley accused Rousseau of taking refuge in the technique of typical schoolmen who assume that the mere analysis of terms is the accurate approach to acquiring fresh truths. Much of Rousseau's writing, he said, is reducible to "mere logical deductions from verbal definitions, which the slightest attempt to confront with actual fact would have shown to be not only valueless, but wholly meaningless, in connection with real human nature and the visible working of human affairs."[9] Rousseau is guilty of peering into a word, injecting his own verbal notion into it, and informing his reader about his discovery. He should have been concerned with the object denoted by the term. He raises questions that are not necessarily false but are not worthwhile raising, and utilizes this means as a technique for extracting meaning from a verbal notion rather than ascertaining whether the idea does indeed correspond to fact. "Rousseau was always apt to think in a slipshod manner, and sensibly though illogically accepted wholesome practical maxims, as if they flowed from theoretical premises that were in truth utterly incompatible with them."[10]

II *Comments by Harald Höffding*

The distinguished professor of philosophy at the University of Copenhagen, Harald Höffding (1843-1931), presented several critical comments on Rousseau's philosophy of education in his *Jean Jacques Rousseau and His Philosophy*. Höffding objected to Rousseau's contention in the *Emile* that the poor man requires little or no education, the presupposition being that it is reserved mainly for the children of the wealthy. For Rousseau, who is presumably the prophet of democracy, it is an aristocratic trait that does not become him. He did advocate free public education in his *Considerations on the Government of Poland and on Its Proposed Reformation* in 1772, but in general it remained for Pestalozzi, Rousseau's disciple, to extend his mentor's views by bringing education to the common people. Thus Rousseau's point of view had to be supplemented and corrected by Pestalozzi, Basedow, and other followers.

Rousseau, fearful of stimulating the emotions and imaginations of children prematurely, deferred this aspect of their development until the period of adolescence. Höffding objected to the argument that such training should await the development of the child's reasoning powers and to Rousseau's advice: Better too late than too soon.

This is perhaps the most dubious point in Rousseau's theory of education, a point in which he contradicts himself, since he insists upon the very importance and the independence of the emotions. Negative education should only provide the nourishment and development for the feeling and imagination proper to the stage of the child's development; yet Rousseau would cut these off from all nourishment. Herein his reaction to his own past, and also the sophistry of his own doctrines, carried him too far.[11]

There appears to be little basis, according to Höffding, for the idea that developing the imagination too soon would be accompanied by premature sexual experience.

Like Morley, Höffding severely criticized Rousseau's views on the education of women, whom he regarded as different from men in their natural structure, temperament, and character, and therefore requiring a different educational program. Höffding deprecated the emphasis upon natural functions of wifehood and motherhood as the basis for education in meekness and submissiveness. He rejected Rousseau's assumptions that a married woman's intellectual powers suffice only to select practical means toward a given goal but not the goal itself and that, since her husband determines the goal for her, she must adopt his religious beliefs and obey him as her valid authority without question. The father's authority over an unmarried daughter is similarly denied.

Höffding pointed out that Rousseau, misled by the prejudices of his culture into assigning an inferior role to women, then inexplicably contradicted himself by ascribing to women "a natural talent to rule over man." This dubious power of women is to be exercised in accordance with Rousseau's exhortation that properly "the rule of woman is a rule of mildness, of tact, and of amiability; her commands are caresses, her threats are tears."[12] Rousseau never succeeded in resolving this contradiction, "for the great practical influence he attributes to woman becomes a very questionable one if she cannot go through an independent spiritual development that allows her to gain insight, at first hand, into the 'aims' as well as the 'means,' into the 'principles' as well as the 'details.' "[13] If Rousseau had accorded girls the same educational rights as boys, if he had carefully studied the special nature of women before formulating pedagogical rules for them, he would have become well aware of their talents and needs worthy of every natural right to development. Hence it was quite accurate for Morley to refer to Rousseau's conception of woman as "oriental." Rousseau made the mistake of accepting a cultural distortion of his time instead of following his own advice to take the cue from nature.

Höffding nevertheless held that Rousseau's system of

educational philosophy is fundamentally consistent even though it created perplexing problems, and he reminded us that raising problems may often merit higher praise than solving them. Rousseau certainly raised serious problems. Aware that society requires certain patterns of behavior and adjustment on the part of the individual, in his later writings he modified his protest against his contemporary civilization. He even made a distinction between a natural type of civilization evolving out of individual and social experience and an artificial type of culture that is imposed upon men without regard for their individual development and effort. "The great problem—which Rousseau raised with more sense than the critics have usually recognized, the problem which in its several forms took up his whole soul, as a pedagogical, a psychological, and a social writer—he did not solve."[14]

III *Wright's Evaluation*

Ernest Hunter Wright of Columbia University in his *The Meaning of Rousseau* attempted to determine what Rousseau really meant by his frequently inconsistent or apparently contradictory statements. Owing to his inconsistency, Rousseau's ideas have become the subject of divergent interpretations and heated disputes among philosophers and educators.

A typical basic discrepancy relates to Rousseau's advocacy of a return to nature as a means of human education and betterment.

Four men out of five will say that when Rousseau tells us to return to nature, he means us to give up all the hard-won gains of culture and get back to savagery or animality. Voltaire implied as much in his ironical confession that Rousseau made him itch to go on all fours; and down to our day a host of critics far less nimble-jointed have kept finding the same admonition in our author and greeting it with every exhibition of amazement, spleen, or horror. But other critics tell us that Rousseau means no such thing; that he never once says it, but repeatedly denies it; and that far from pleading with us to go back to savagery, he is imploring us to press on to a higher culture than any we have known. Why is it that we read such opposite meanings in him?[15]

Is it possible that both interpretations are correct because Rousseau's work is contradictory, a mere "quilt of shreds and patches?" For example, the advice Rousseau offered in *Emile* is not what he prescribed for the children of Poland. He dismisses property as virtually the root of all evil, and then in a turnabout sees it as a sacred institution. In one breath he offers a plea for individual liberty and then advocates complete submission to the state. While proclaiming tolerance for all men, he demands the expulsion of all atheists from the republic. At one time he becomes democracy's pernicious leveller, at another the proud aristocrat; or a reformer who looks backward and a revolutionist afraid to move forward. Wright cited such inconsistencies as reasons why so many opposing contradictory movements can trace their origins to Rousseau.

One point that Wright and other critics conceded is the beautiful lucidity of Rousseau's style; he avoids abstruse arguments and metaphysical contortions; that is, he is quite readable. Wright pointed out that Rousseau was attempting to be a poet and a philosopher at the same time in a period when combining poetry and philosophy was an antiquated notion. "Rousseau has the dubious gift of epigram, and loves to fling off now and then a kind of paradox that remains unforgettable when all the context that explains and mitigates it is forgotten. Thus every one remembers his saying that 'the man who meditates is a degenerate animal.' "[16] Critics have seized upon such remarks as the essence of Rousseau's philosophy, but to do so is to commit the fallacy of vicious abstraction. This is not to assert, however, that every element of Rousseau's philosophy is harmoniously integrated to the point of perfection.

Had Rousseau provided a synopsis of his first principles, considerable confusion would have been obviated. Instead, such information must be assembled from his helter-skelter arrangement. Trouble would also have been avoided had he been consistent in his use and definition of terms, i.e., had he used one and the same word to convey one and the same meaning. "He could have spared us a good deal, at moments when he was inexorably pushing logic on disparate problems to conclusions equally disparate, if he had admitted the discrepancies and shown a reason for them, and a higher unity when possible."[17] The contradictions encountered by Rousseau often result from his transferring from one universe of discourse to quite another. For example, he could have avoided a contradiction simply by asserting that the first person who seized a portion of property introduced a multiplicity of evil into society, but that in an ideal state legal provision for property ownership can be a beneficent and sacred right. It is possible that he thought that this was the idea he conveyed, but his critics maintain that, if such had been his view, he should have stated it more clearly.

Sometimes the appearance of confusion and shifting from one universe of discourse to another are not attributable to Rousseau but to his critics. Specific groups of critics may disagree in their interpretations; for instance, the universe of discourse of the philosopher may be quite different from that of the anthropologist or the economist. Specialists from varied disciplines could be responsible for the "vast confusion of tongues." The idea of natural man, for example, may convey a different meaning to a philosopher, psychologist, political scientist, educator, anthropologist, theologian, and literary critic, hence the varied meanings possible for a single term and its concomitant confusion. Moreover, some critics cannot find truth in Rousseau merely because they do not care to do so. Rather than glorify him, they prefer to vilify him, the reason being that he is unpleasant and rips the mask from the educational, political, moral, and religious prejudices of people.

IV Analysis by William Boyd

William Boyd, of the University of Glasgow, underscored the inconsistencies of Rousseau. He noted Rousseau's contradictory assertions that all education like any other social contrivance is contrary to nature, but that a good education is possible provided that society itself be regenerated. Had Rousseau not added the second assertion, he would have had nothing useful to say about education. Despite his negative attitude toward society, Rousseau nevertheless believed that social institutions could be brought into conformity with nature. Once that result had been achieved, ideal education would be feasible.

In the first book of the *Emile,* Rousseau lamented the fact that education was no longer viable owing to the unworthiness of the states which were being embraced as their fatherland by the loyal citizens. A state fostering natural education is one in which a citizen can invest his life completely, as was the case with the city-states of the ancient Greeks. Boyd held that individuality is drowned in monstrously large modern countries so that natural education of the kind described in the *Emile* becomes an impossibility, a conclusion which Rousseau himself reached even though he inconsistently envisioned the possibility of educating boys for society under ideal conditions so that they would become, not unnatural persons, but true men and good citizens.

V *Objections of Gabriel Compayré*

Gabriel Compayré, Director of the Academy of Lyon and Correspondent of the Institute, emphasized inconsistencies in Rousseau's philosophy of education. He commented: "Paradox begets paradox, and from the erroneous principle which serves as a starting-point of *Emile* has sprung the entire series of pedagogical falsities, for which Rousseau has been so severely but so justly reproved, what Nisard called his 'enormities,' and the English pedagogue, R. Hebert Quick, 'his extravaganzas.' "[18] The paradoxes and contradictions in Rousseau's works have been widely scored by Compayré and other eminent scholars.

Compayré objected to Rousseau's advocacy of a doubly negative education designed to educate both without discipline and without instruction. He felt that this point of view was too extreme and that a happy compromise should be sought between a total lack of discipline and an excessive severity, referring to the "tender insinuations of a mother's affection or the injunctions of a father's strong will, at once gentle and firm, or the persuasive exhortations of a kindly and watchful master."[19] How ironic, noted Compayré, that

Rousseau's impassionate plea for natural education neglected to allow for one of nature's strongest bent, the authority of parents—for even animals control their young.

VI *Favorable Reactions of Alfred Cobban*

According to Alfred Cobban, virtually all modern literary criticism of Rousseau is derived from H. Taine, who wrote his multivolume *Les origines de la France contemporaine* in 1875, which included the important first volume, *L'ancien régime.* "With Brunetière it becomes more acute, and with some modern critics inconceivably shrill and bitter,"[20] the reason being that their religious feelings tended to aggravate their political opposition to Rousseau's philosophy. Ordinarily a writer encounters the greatest hostility among his contemporary critics, but, said Cobban, the reason that Rousseau remains a major target is that "his literary conquests are among the greatest, the most vulnerable and the most triumphantly inexpugnable of all the achievements of French romanticism."[21] It still offends many critics that Rousseau created a wide gap between the point of view he represented and that of the eighteenth-century mind.

Cobban defended Rousseau from those critics who charge that the great French philosopher was guilty of a "mass of contradictions to which chronology affords the only key." If Rousseau's works are so replete with contradictions, why do these scholars devote so much of their time and effort to detailed analysis of his philosophy? One might ponder whether Rousseau, from their point of view, is worth studying at all!

Rousseau's major inconsistency is the discrepancy between the ideals he espoused and the life he led, a contradiction receiving the greatest attention from his critics. Yet there is a defence for Rousseau; it does not seem fair to blame a person for the sins of his youth in view of his assertion of a quite different point of view and more thoughtful deliberation in his maturity. It is possible indeed for Rousseau to have experienced a complete transformation in moral character; at least in his writings Rousseau faced up to his contradictions and became his own severest critic.

A modus operandi common to certain critics of Rousseau

consists of abstracting isolated statements which, when removed from their context, appear strikingly contradictory. Logicians refer to this technique as the fallacy of vicious abstraction. Rousseau himself protested against this unfair method of reducing his system to fragmented bits by less than honest critics who had the impudence to charge him with immorality.

Cobban objected to the practice of some critics in treating Rousseau as if he were an adherent to an academic tradition of abstract theory. Instead of belonging to any such tradition, he created a new departure by means of his truly original ideas. In politics, education, ethics, and literature he was always to be found at the entrance of the great philosophical pathway leading to our own times.

The primary reason for studying Rousseau is to clarify the historical origins and development of his viable educational and political ideas and their effects upon future generations. "These general conceptions," wrote Cobban, "that play such a great part in history, are those most in need of the conscious analysis and illustration that only the genius who understands and shares them can provide. Rousseau is worth studying, if only because in him can be clearly seen for the first time so many of our own accepted ideas, and because the essential nature of an idea is often most manifest in its beginnings."[22] The worthwhile truths commanding the attention of the historian are not recondite academic doctrines bandied about from theorist to theorist, but the "truths of the marketplace."

VII *A Few Conclusions*

Curious, is it not, that despite Rousseau's great concern for living according to nature and educating according to what is natural, his critics did not challenge Rousseau's concept of the natural? In this respect, one glaring shortcoming of Rousseau that has been brought to light by modern anthropologists like Margaret Mead and Ruth Benedict is his neglect of the social and cultural determinants of personality; e.g., sexual and other roles generally considered to be innate have been shown instead to be cultural to a consider-

able extent. Not that culture is the sole factor in forming
personality, for heredity, individual differences, and physiol-
ogy play a part. In her researches among the people of
Manus in New Guinea, Mead found that temperament and
disposition were culturally induced. While Freud's
psychoanalytical views regarding the dominance and aggres-
siveness of the male and the recessiveness of the female
agree with Rousseau's so closely that one might ask whether
Freud was influenced by Rousseau, Mead's position is in
striking contrast to the views of both thinkers. She concluded that the behavior of the male and the female could be
explained in terms of culture, with society as the determin-
ant of proper male and female patterns of behavior. Whereas
Rousseau was quite right in arguing that education accounts
for forming personalities, he was in error in attributing male
and female cultural differences to nature rather than to society. Not the forces of nature, but education and cultural development during the early period of one's life form his personality traits. Human nature, being exceedingly malleable,
responds readily to deliberately planned influences which result in the shaping and modification of behavior patterns and
the acquisition of desirable personality characteristics.

Of course, native equipment cannot be disregarded. Notwithstanding the arguments of some adherents to the
women's liberation movement, for example, the attempt to
reduce all individuals to a unisex, with the masculine sex as
the working paradigm, would be a most dubious extreme ex-
pedient. Women can be liberated without surrendering their
sex, or altering their personalities to resemble that of the
male. Marcuse has rightly held that "this equalization of
male and female would be regressive: it would be a new form
of female acceptance of a male principle."[23] Rousseau was in
a sense justified in assigning different personalities to men
and women, though he was undoubtedly in error (a victim of
his time and culture) in the personalities that he assigned to
men and women, for he attributed them to innate predispositions foreordained by nature.

Another point at issue is Rousseau's assumption that what
is natural is *eo ipso* good. To accept nature at face value is

absurd, for man's animalistic aggressions would play havoc with the lives of others. "In sober truth," asserted John Stuart Mill, "nearly all the things which men are hanged or imprisoned for doing to one another are nature's everyday performances."[24] Many of those accomplishments of the human race that are desirable run counter to nature, if by nature is meant allowing natural forces to follow their course without human intervention. If men and women did not intervene, then many dread diseases subject to therapy would take their natural course, devastating masses of people with pain and premature death.

Moreover, since human intelligence is as natural as any other human attribute, the suitable application of intelligence would mean the desirable modification of many other natural tendencies. The great philosopher Francis Bacon reminded us that people can obey nature in such a way as to be in command of it.

To speak of a *natural* process in control of events connotes either that (1) the entire universe must remain exactly as it stands, or (2) things in nature must proceed on their course without human intervention. If the first conclusion is accepted, then people must do what is natural willy-nilly, for nothing else is within their power. If the second meaning is accepted, then immorality and irrationality result. Mill said:

The doctrine that man ought to follow nature or, in other words, ought to make the spontaneous course of things the model of his voluntary actions is equally irrational and immoral:

Irrational, because all human action whatever consists in altering, and all useful action in improving, the spontaneous course of nature.

Immoral, because the course of natural phenomena being replete with everything which when committed by human beings is most worthy of abhorrence, anyone who endeavored in his actions to imitate the natural course of things would be universally seen and acknowledged to be the wickedest of men.[25]

What, then, should one's obligations be with respect to the natural? A person should co-operate with natural powers by constantly attempting to upgrade the course of nature, bringing nature into closer conformity with the highest values of which mankind is aware, i.e., to exercise such control over nature that it becomes more attuned to goodness.

If nature were invariably right and infallible, then Darwin's theory of the survival of the fittest would be the appropriate ethic to adopt. But even Darwin did not accept natural processes as the basis for ethics, preferring sympathy and conscience (as Rousseau did) instead. T. H. Huxley argued that it is not the natural course that should be promoted, but the course that ought to survive or is morally worthy of survival. Huxley perceived two courses in the universe: the cosmic process and the ethical process. He contended that

Social progress means a checking of the cosmic process at every step and the substitution for it of another, which may be called the ethical process; the end of which is not the survival of those who may happen to be the fittest, in respect of the whole of the conditions which obtain, but of those who are ethically the best.[26]

A person's paramount duty, then, is to employ his intellect in service to humanity. Survival of the fittest should therefore signify the morally fittest. Huxley went on to say: "Let us understand, once for all, that the ethical progress of society depends, not on imitating the cosmic process, still less in running away from it, but in combatting it."[27] Note what is done in horticulture; it is not any old weed that is permitted to grow but only those plants deemed beautiful and worthy of cultivation. The same is true in the human world, for it is not any impulse that should be allowed to be expressed but only those impulses contributing to the harmony, beauty, and goodness of the world.

What, then, did Rousseau mean by the term, *natural*? He meant all of these things and more; he meant whatever served his purpose. Never explicit or precise in his uses of this term, he often used it to signify whatever he wanted it to mean. Occasionally he meant by it instinctive urges, but instinct is hardly an acceptable criterion of truth. Instincts are vague concepts that are ill-defined. Imagine the lot of humanity if the race had to accept instinct as its main test of truth! All science and knowledge would come to a complete standstill; medical, engineering, and other sciences would be unknown. If man obeyed his instincts and not his intellect, he would have no knowledge of space and would still be earth-bound, and, in fact, instinct is not even suitable as a guide in the sphere of animalistic appetite, for it certainly does not help us to eat the proper foods containing the most suitable nutrients, nor does it warn us when over-eating is unhealthy. If men and animals depended only upon instincts, the animals would fare better than the human beings.

As a champion of individual liberty, Rousseau became the great destroyer of tradition and preferred sentiment to reason as a guide to education. He was criticized for personal immorality and philosophical inconsistency, but he swept down like a hurricane upon his society of artificial restraints, ancient superstitions, and intellectual and materialistic poverty, restriction, and turmoil. Himself egotistic, unreliable, immoral, and inconsistent, this Jekyll-Hyde genius was also humane, nature-loving, logical, courageous, frank and fair, a noble person worthy of sympathy. Critics condemned him as a destructive force but it must be admitted that the destruction of evil and the breaking of chains are truly constructive steps clearing the road to progress.

What are the implications of Rousseau's basic ideas for contemporary education? Surely his emphasis on nature study and natural impulses is a significant contribution. Although in a sense all education is natural inasmuch as man is himself part of nature, education must take into account the native equipment of the individual from the period of birth onward if it is to be effective. Surely, too, education should follow Rousseau's stress upon the necessity for spontaneous activity, physical and sensory training, and practical life experience. It is not necessary to accept his extreme condemnation of symbolic or abstract learning, for concern with practical activities may often neglect the real meaning of experiences, and, for best results, imaginative minds require abstract generalizations and symbolic inspiration, yet learning from active experience is essential. We need not condemn, as Rousseau did, all the institutions of society, for man is a social as well as a private person and should not be isolated from community influences, but the needs and characteristics of the individual must have primary consideration. As Rousseau insisted, enjoyment and happiness in activity are indispensable ingredients of good educational programs. Even in the weakest portion of Rousseau's conception of education, that relating to the training of women for domestic duties and a life of subservience to men, there is some degree of truth worthy of analysis. Rousseau failed to recognize the real nature of woman, which includes all the social, physical, and psychological attributes of the human being as such, but there is something to be learned from his respect for wifehood and motherhood as the most vital functions of most women which should not be altogether ignored in our own time of well-balanced coeducational education.

Finally, parents and teachers would do well to heed Rousseau's wise admonitions concerning the power of adult example to mold the characters of children. If adults are overtly or covertly corrupt, aggressive, and lawless, then, irrespective of other educational influences, how can they expect children to develop integrity, mutual regard, and self-control or self-direction as law-abiding citizens? If the sore thumbs of society are to be healed, if the imperfect institutions and defective or immoral practices condemned by discerning critics today, as they were by the great French educator in his own time, are to be properly treated and rectified, educational therapy must begin at both ends of the lifespan and be applied especially to young adults as well, for the power of Rousseau's good model is essential to the improvement of human nature and creation of that ideal human being, that natural man, of his *Emile*.

Notes and References

Chapter 1

1. *The Confessions,* bk. 1.
2. *Ibid.*
3. *Ibid.*
4. *Ibid.*
5. *Reveries, 10.*
6. *The Confessions,* bk. 2.
7. *Ibid.*
8. *Ibid.,* bk. 3.

Chapter 2

1. *Emile,* bk. 1.
2. *Discourse on the Origin and the Foundations of Inequality among Men,* introduction to pt. 1.
3. *Emile,* bk. 2.
4. Thomas Hobbes, *Leviathan,* pt. 1, ch. 13.
5. *Discourse on the Origin and the Foundations of Inequality among Men,* pt. 1.
6. *Ibid.*
7. *Emile,* bk. 2.
8. *Ibid.,* bk. 4.
9. *Ibid.,* bk. 1.
10. *Ibid.,* bk. 4.
11. *Discourse on the Origin and the Foundations of Inequality among Men,* pt. 2.
12. *Emile,* bk. 4.
13. *Discourse on the Origin and the Foundations of Inequality among Men,* appendix.

14. *Discourse on the Sciences and the Arts,* pt. 1.

15. *Ibid.,* pt. 2.

16. *Ibid.*

17. *Ibid.*

18. *Ibid.*

19. *Discourse on the Origin and the Foundations of Inequality among Men,* pt. 2.

20. *Ibid.*

21. *Ibid.,* appendix.

22. *Emile,* bk. 2.

23. *Ibid.*

24. *Ibid.*

25. *The Social Contract,* bk 1, ch. 4.

26. *Ibid.*

27. *Ibid.,* bk. 2., ch. 8.

Chapter 3

1. "Political Economy," in the *Encyclopédie.* Translated and included in William Boyd (ed.), *The Minor Educational Writings of Jean Jacques Rousseau* (New York: Teachers College, Columbia University, 1962), p. 41.

2. *Ibid.,* pp. 41-42.

3. *Ibid.,* p. 41.

4. *Considerations on the Government of Poland.* Translated and included in F. M. Watkins (ed.), *Rousseau: Political Writings* (New York: Nelson, 1953), ch. 4.

5. *Ibid.*

6. *Ibid.*

7. *The Project for the Education of M. de Sainte-Marie.* Translated and included in William Boyd (ed.), *The Minor Educational Writings of Jean Jacques Rousseau* (New York: Teachers College, Columbia University, 1962), p. 28.

8. *Ibid.,* p. 29.

9. *Ibid.,* p. 31.

10. *Ibid.,* p. 33.

11. John Locke, *An Essay concerning Human Understanding,* bk. 2, ch. 1.

12. *Ibid.,* bk. 4. ch. 19.

13. John Locke, *Some Thoughts concerning Education,* 1693 (Cambridge: Cambridge University Press, 1884), sect. 60.

14. *Ibid.,* sect. 66.

15. *Ibid.,* sect. 69.

16. *Ibid.*
17. *Ibid.*, sect. 72.
18. *Ibid.*, sect. 148.
19. *Ibid.*, sect. 89.
20. *Ibid.*, sect. 66.
21. *Ibid.*
22. Philippe Ariès, *Centuries of Childhood: A Social History of Family Life* (New York: Alfred A Knopf, 1962), pp. 29-30.
23. *Ibid.*, p. 119.

Chapter 4

1. *The Confessions*, bk. 10.
2-6. Quotations from *New Heloise*, pt. 3, letter 1.
7-39. Quotations from *New Heloise, Ibid.*, pt. 5, letter 3.

Chapter 5

1-21. Quotations from *Emile*, bk. 1.
22-51. Quotations from *Emile*, bk. 2.
52-66. Quotations from *Emile*, bk. 3.
67-91. Quotations from *Emile*, bk. 4.
92. "Extracts from Three Letters to the Abbé M.," in William Boyd (ed.), *The Minor Educational Writings of Jean Jacques Rousseau* (New York: Teachers College, Columbia University, 1962), p. 88.

Chapter 6

1-24. Quotations from *Emile*, bk. 5.
25. "Memoir on the Education of the Prince of Wirtemberg's Infant Daughter, Sophie" (1763), in William Boyd (ed.), *The Minor Educational Writings of Jean Jacques Rousseau* (New York: Teachers College, Columbia University, 1962), pp. 78, 82, 83.

Chapter 7

1. Johann Christoph Friedrich Schiller, "Rousseau." Translated by Peter Gay and included as part of his "introduction" to Ernest Cassirer, *The Question of Jean-Jacques Rousseau* (Bloomington: Indiana University Press, 1963), p. 5.
2. Immanuel Kant, *Education* (Ann Arbor, Michigan: University of Michigan Press, 1960), pp. 87-88.

3. Paul Merrill Spurlin, *Rousseau in America: 1760-1809* (University, Alabama: University of Alabama Press, 1969), p. 110.
4. *Ibid.,* p. 113.

Chapter 8

1. John Morley, *Rousseau* (London: Chapman and Hall, 1873), II, p. 122.
2. *Ibid.,* pp. 122-123.
3. *Ibid.,* II, p. 214-215.
4. *Ibid.,* pp. 228-229.
5. *Ibid.,* p. 243.
6. *Ibid.,* p. 248.
7. *Ibid.,* p. 126.
8. *Ibid.,* p. 134.
9. *Ibid.,* pp. 135-136.
10. *Ibid.,* I, p. 192.
11. Harald Höffding, *Jean Jacques Rousseau and His Philosophy* (New Haven: Yale University Press, 1930), pp. 151-152.
12. *Emile,* bk. 5.
13. Harald Höffding, *Jean Jacques Rousseau and His Philosophy* (New Haven: Yale University Press, 1930), pp. 155-156.
14. *Ibid.,* p. xxiv.
15. Ernest Hunter Wright, *The Meaning of Rousseau* (Oxford: Oxford University Press, 1929). (Reissued, New York: Russell & Russell, 1963), p. 1.
16. *Ibid.,* p. 3.
17. *Ibid.,* p. 4.
18. Gabriel Compayré, *Jean Jacques Rousseau and Education from Nature* (New York: Thomas Y. Crowell, 1907), p. 24.
19. *Ibid.,* p. 26.
20. Alfred Cobban, *Rousseau and the Modern State* (London: George Allen & Unwin, 1934), p. 40.
21. *Ibid.*
22. *Ibid.,* p. 22.
23. Herbert Marcuse, *Counterrevolution and Revolt* (Boston: Beacon Press, 1972), p. 78.
24. John Stuart Mill, *Nature* (London: Longmans, Green, 1875).
25. *Ibid.*
26. Thomas Henry Huxley, *Evolution and Ethics,* 1893.
27. *Ibid.*

Selected Bibliography of Rousseau's Writings

With Special Emphasis on His Philosophy of Education

(1736) Letter to His Father. (Concerns his choice of a vocation.)

(1740) Project for the Education of M. de Sainte-Marie. (Details and defends his philosophy of education.)

(1749) Memoir for M. Dupin.

(1750) *Discourse on the Sciences and the Arts.* (Discussion of the effects of sciences and arts on customs and morals.)

(1755) *Discourse on the Origin and the Foundations of Inequality among Men.* (Advocacy of return to nature as remedy for political inequality. Differences in education contribute to inequality.)

(1755) "Political Economy" in *Encyclopédie.* (Education for selfless citizenship.)

(1758) *Discourse on Political Economy.* (Preview of *The Social Contract.*)

(1758) *Letter to M. d'Alembert on the Theatre.* (Comments on d'Alembert's article, "Genève," in the seventh volume of the *Encyclopédie.*)

(1758) Letter to Dr. Tronchin (November 27). (Discusses public education of Geneva's citizens.)

(1759) Letter to Madame de Créqui (January 15). (Treats the education of her son.)

(1761) *Julie, or the New Heloise.* (Second in importance only to *Emile* as source of information about Rousseau's views on education. Letter 3 in part 5 is especially rich in his philosophy of education.)

(1762) *Emile.* (Rousseau's classic on the philosophy of education.)

(1762) *The Social Contract.* (Rousseau's classic on political philosophy; also important for an understanding of his philosophy of education.)

(1763) Letter to Monsignor de Beaumont, Archbishop of Paris. (Rousseau's response to the archbishop's condemnation of his *Emile.*)

(1763-1764) Letters to the Prince of Wirtemberg concerning his infant daughter's education. (Letters dated January 21, September 3, November 20, and December 15 are of particular value to the philosophy of education.)

(1764) Letters on the Mount.

(1767) Dictionary of Music. (A work reflecting Rousseau's limited knowledge of music and musical instruction.)

(1770) Letters to the Abbé M. (Letters dated February 9, February 28, and March 14.)

(1771) Letter to Madame de T. (Letter of April 6, discussing difficulties encountered in her child's education.)

(1772) *Considerations on the Government of Poland and on Its Proposed Reformation.* (Chapter 4 is rich in information about Rousseau's philosophy of education as a basis for state educational programs.)

(1776) *Rousseau juge de Jean-Jacques.* (Rousseau, Judge of Jean-Jacques. Rousseau discusses *Emile* in the context of his other writings.)

(1780) *Emile and Sophie.*

(1782-1789) *The Confessions.* (The first chapters of this autobiography contain Rousseau's recollections of his own early education. Book 6 describes his experiences as tutor to the sons of M. de Mably.)

Selected Bibliography of Secondary Sources in English

BABBITT, IRVING. *Rousseau and Romanticism*. Boston, 1919.

BLANCHARD, WILLIAM H. *Rousseau and the Spirit of Revolt: A Psychological Study*. Ann Arbor, Michigan, 1967.

BOYD, WILLIAM. *The Educational Theory of Jean Jacques Rousseau*. New York, 1963.

BROOME, J. H. *Rousseau: A Study of His Thought*. London, 1963.

GAY, PETER. *The Question of Jean-Jacques Rousseau*. Bloomington, Indiana, 1963.

CHARPENTIER, JOHN. *Rousseau: The Child of Nature*. New York, 1931.

COBBAN, ALFRED. *Rousseau and the Modern State*. London, 1934.

COBBAN, ALFRED. *In Search of Humanity: The Role of the Enlightenment in Modern History*. London, 1960.

COMPAYRÉ, GABRIEL. *Jean Jacques Rousseau and Education from Nature*. New York, 1907.

CROCKER, LESTER G. *Rousseau's Social Contract: An Interpretive Essay*. Cleveland, 1968.

DAVIDSON, THOMAS. *Rousseau and Education according to Nature*. New York, 1898.

ELLIS, MADELEINE B. *Rousseau's Venetian Story: An Essay upon Art and Truth in Les Confessions*. Baltimore, 1966.

GREEN, F. C. *Jean-Jacques Rousseau: A Critical Study of His Life and Writings*. Cambridge, 1955.

GRIMSLEY, RONALD. "Rousseau, Jean-Jacques," *Encyclopedia of Philosophy*. New York, 1967, VII, 218-225.

GUÉHENNO, JEAN. *Jean-Jacques Rousseau*. 2 Vols. London, 1966.

HENDEL, CHARLES WILLIAM. *Jean-Jacques Rousseau: Moralist*. 2 Vols. London, 1934.

147

HÖFFDING, HARALD. *Jean Jacques Rousseau and His Philosophy.* New Haven, 1930.

JOSEPHSON, MATTHEW. *Jean-Jacques Rousseau.* New York, 1931.

MACDONALD, FREDERIKE. *Studies in the France of Voltaire and Rousseau.* London, 1895.

MCDONALD, JOAN. *Rousseau and the French Revolution: 1762-1791.* London, 1965.

MORLEY, JOHN. *Rousseau.* 2 Vols. London, 1873.

SPURLIN, PAUL MERRILL. *Rousseau in America: 1760-1809.* University, Alabama, 1969.

WINWAR, FRANCES. *Jean-Jacques Rousseau: Conscience of an Era.* New York, 1961.

WRIGHT, ERNEST HUNTER. *The Meaning of Rousseau.* Oxford, 1929.

Index

Abelard, P., 63
Academy of Sciences, 23
Adams, J., 122
Adolescents, 57, 59; education of, 98-103
d'Alembert, 24
Alps, 19
An Essay concerning Human Understanding, 53, 57
Annecy, 22
Antirationalism, 32
Aristotelian philosophy, 95
Art of forming men, 78-106
Authority, 44

Basedow, J. B., 120
Basile, 19-20
Benedict, R., 135
Bernard (Rousseau's uncle), 11, 17
Boarding school, 59
Body politic, 42-43
Bomton, 63 ff.
Boyd, W., 132, 133

Capacity, 71
de la Chalotais, R., 60
Chambéry, 11
Channing, W. E., 122
Character education, 71-74, 76
Childhood education, 38-40, 48-52, 58, 86-93
Civilization, 29

Cobban, A., 134, 135
Coddling children, 58
Condillac, E. B. de, 49, 105
Confessions, The, 12, 15, 20, 24, 26, 57, 121
Conscience, 31-32, 112
Considerations on the Government of Poland, 46-48, 128
Contract, social, 30

Darwin, C., 138
Developmental stages of education, 80-81
Devin du village, 11
Diderot, 24
Dijon, 24
Discourse on Political Economy, 121
Discourse on the Origin and the Foundations of Inequality among Men, 11, 24, 28
Discourse on the Sciences and the Arts, 11, 24, 28
Disposition, 114
Ducommun, 17, 18
Dupin, 23
Duty, 72, 89

Education, 33-38; according to nature, 42-60, 66 ff.; adolescent, 98-103; as art of forming men, 78-106; as divine endeavor, 104; as re-education, 35-38; by book of nature, 55; by

rules, 54, 115-17; character, 71-74, 76; childhood, 38-40, 48-52, 58, 86-93; developmental stages of, 80-81; Emile's, 78-106; for citizenship, 46; infant, 81-86; Latin, 60; male, 78-106; national, 46-48; negative, 33-35, 133; of women, 107-117; pre-adolescent, 93-97; reading, 71; reform, 88; religious, 77, 110-12; role of, 33-34; rule of, 90; sex, 39-40, 58, 99-100; trade, 95-96
Educational reform, 88
Effeminateness, 96
Emile, 12, 25, 26, 27, 28, 32, 60, 78-106, 118, 126, 140
Encyclopedia (French), 42
Eudaimonism, 95
Enjoyment, 140
Enlightenment period, 53, 56-57
d'Épinay, 25
Ermenonville, 12

Faculty, 71
Female education, 107-109
Feminity, importance of, 108
Fenelon, 56
Fontainebleau, 25
Freedom, 40-41, 97, 106, 118
Freud, S., 136
Froebel, F., 120

Games, 109; coeducational, 109
General will, 42
Geneva, 11, 17, 23
God, 104
Goodness, as innate, 34
de Gouvon, 21
Gratien, B., 59
Growth stages, 75-76
Gulliver's Travels, 122

Hall, D., 122
Happiness, 101, 121, 140; as absence of pain, 95; as negative, 95; as supreme goal, 95; characteristics of, 95; moral, 95
Heloise, 63
History, 91
Hobbes, T., 29, 30

Höffding, H., 128, 129
Hume, D., 12
d'Huodetot, 25
Huxley, T. H., 138

Ignorance, 51, 94
Immorality, 44-45
Immortality, 87
Individual differences, 67-71
Individualism, 41
Indoctrination, religious, 19
Infallibility of nature, 138
Infant education, 81-86
Integrity, 51
Intelligence, 51
Irrationalism, 32

Jesuit School, 60
Julie, or the New Heloise, 25, 61-77, 78

Kant, I., 120-21
Knowledge, 52
Kretschmer, E., 70

Lambercier, 17
Latin, 60
Lausanne, 22
Le Maitre, 22
Les Charmettres, 23
Les Muse Galantes, 11
Lessing, 120
Letters on the Mount, 26
Letter to d'Alembert on the Theater, 25
Liberty, 40-41, 45, 121
Library, 52
Locke, J., 49, 52, 53, 55, 56, 57, 84, 105, 123
Love, 29-31, 36, 98-99, 114, 116

Male education, 78-106
Manual labor, 95-96
Marcuse, H., 136
Marriage, 114
Mead, M., 135
Mill, J. S., 137
Milord Edward, 63 ff.
Montaigne, 56, 57, 58
Montlouis, 25
Montpellier, 11, 23

Moral, 51, 121; discrimination, 102; happiness, 95
Morley, J., 123, 124, 125, 126, 127, 129

Natural, 118, 138; as criterion of good, 27-41; education, 42-60, 66 ff.; meaning of, 28-29; stages of growth, 75-76
Negative education, 33-35, 133
Neuchâtel, 22
Neuhof, 120
New Heloise, 12, 25, 121, 122

Of Civil Government, 53
Original sin, 34
Ovid, 16

Paris, 22, 23
Pascal, B., 64
Passions, 98-99
Peace, 102
Pedagogue, 58
Personality, 113; development, 71
Pestalozzi, J. H., 120, 128
Philosophy, 23
Plato, 33, 70, 105
Plutarch, 16
"Political Economy", 42
de Pontverre, 18
Port Royal, 59
Port Royalists, 23
Pre-adolescent education, 93-97
Prejudice, 104
Pride, 36, 46
"Profession of the Vicar of Savoy", 61
Project for the Education of M. de Sante-Marie, 49-52, 54
Prudence, 87
Psychology, 71-74; of adolescence, 57

Reason, 32-33, 100; role of, 32-33
Recreation, 51
Religion, 34, 51, 62; Christian, 34
Religious education, 77, 110-12
Reveries, 26
Reward, 51
Richardson, S., 61
Robinson Crusoe, 95

Role of education, 33-34
de la Roque, 20
Rousseau, F., 16
Rousseau, J. J., biography, 15-25; birth, 15; childhood, 16-17; criticism of, 123-40; influence of, 118-22; paradoxes of, 133; style of, 131

Rule of education, 90, 115-17

Saint-Preux, 62 ff.
Savage, 33
Savoy, 22
Schiller, 119, 120
Sedentariness, 96
Self-control, 35
Self-love, 29-31, 36, 98
Self-preservation, 86, 98
Sex education, 39-40, 58, 99-100
Shakespeare, W., 122
Slavery, 40, 87
Social Contract, 12, 25, 27, 28, 61, 121, 124
Socialism, 43
Socrates, 33, 119; method of, 110-12
Some Thoughts concerning Education, 52-53, 57
Spurlin, 122
Stages of educational development, 80-81
Stages of growth, 75-76
Stoicism, 38, 41
Sublimation, 39-40
Suffering, 87
Sympathy, 29-31

Tabula rasa mind, 84
Talent, 71
Temperament, 67
Trade, 95
Truth, 51, 53-54, 91
Turin, 19, 21

Values, 104-106; utilitarian, 96
Varro, 50
le Vasseur, T. M., 12, 24
Venice, 11
de Vercellis, 20
Vice, 67-68

Virtue, 32, 44, 68, 125
Voltaire, 11, 23, 25

de Warens, 11, 18-23
Washington, G., 122

Webster, N., 122
de Wolmar, 62 ff.
Women, 125-26; Rousseau's view of,
    125-26
Wright, E. H., 130, 131